Brand Planning for the Pharmaceutical Industry

Brand Planning for the Pharmaceutical Industry

JANICE MacLENNAN

GOWER

Published by
Gower Publishing Limited
Gower House
Croft Road
Aldershot
Hants GU11 3HR
England

Gower Publishing Company
Suite 420
101 Cherry Street
Burlington, VT 05401-4405
USA

British Library Cataloguing in Publication Data
MacLennan, Janice
    Brand planning for the pharmaceutical industry
    1. Drugs – Marketing 2. Brand name products – Planning
    I. Title
    338.4'76151'0688

Library of Congress Cataloging-in-Publication Data
MacLennan, Janice.
    Brand planning for the pharmaceutical industry / Janice MacLennan.
        p. cm.
    ISBN 0-566-08520-8
    1. Drugs--Marketing. 2. Brand name products. 3. Pharmaceutical industry. I. Title.

HD9665.5.M33 2004
615'.1'0688--dc22

                                                    2003068578

Reprinted 2006

ISBN 10: 0 566 08520 8
ISBN 13: 978 0 566 08520 8

Typeset by Sparks, Oxford, UK – www.sparks.co.uk
Printed and bound in Great Britain by MPG Books Ltd, Bodmin, Cornwall

Contents

List of Figures   ix
List of Tables   xi
Acknowledgements   xiii

INTRODUCTION   1
  What is a brand?   1
  Product brand vs. company brand   2
  What is branding?   2
  Is branding important to the pharmaceutical industry?   3
  So why consider branding your products?   3
  An approach to building global brands   4

ABOUT THIS BOOK   7

Part I   **Developing a Brand Plan for a New Product   9**

  1   MARKET SEGMENTATION   11
    What is market segmentation?   11
    Market segmentation – an approach that is necessary for the purposes of brand planning   12
    How to segment a market for the purposes of brand planning   13
    Guidelines for market research   16
    Frequently asked questions   16
    An activity that you might undertake to help you improve your skill at inferring market
        segments (need-states)   17
    Definitions of terms used   17
    Recommended reading   18

  2   EXTERNAL ANALYSIS – THE STARTING POINT   19
    What is meant by 'external analysis'?   19
    What are the deliverables from this analysis?   19
    What are the key ingredients of the external analysis?   20
    How to approach the external analysis   22
    Guidelines for market research   28
    Frequently asked questions   28
    An activity to help you test your skills   29
    Definitions of terms used   30
    Recommended reading   31

3 THE INTERNAL ANALYSIS – THE NEXT STEP   32
   What is the internal analysis?   32
   What are the deliverables from this analysis?   32
   What are the key ingredients of this analysis?   33
   How to approach the internal analysis   33
   Guidelines for market research   38
   Frequently asked questions   40
   An activity to help you test your skills   40
   Definitions of terms used   41
   Recommended reading   42

4 JOINING UP THE THINKING   43
   Why we need joined-up thinking   43
   How to construct the framework for joined-up thinking   44
   How to interpret the joined-up thinking framework   49
   Frequently asked questions   51
   An activity that you might undertake to help you improve your skill   51
   Recommended reading   52

5 FORMULATING THE STRATEGY   53
   What is meant by strategy?   53
   What are the key ingredients in formulating the strategy?   54
   How to approach the development of strategic options   54
   Frequently asked questions   60
   An activity to help you test your skills   60
   Definitions of terms used   61
   Recommended reading   61

6 DEVELOPING THE BRAND STRATEGY   62
   What is meant by brand strategy?   62
   What are the key ingredients in formulating the brand strategy?   63
   Guidelines for writing a brand position statement   65
   How to approach the development of brand strategy   68
   Guidelines for implementing the brand strategy   71
   Guidelines for market research   73
   Frequently asked questions   74
   An activity to help you test your skills   75
   Definitions of terms used   75
   Recommended reading   76

7 COMPLETING THE PLAN   78
   How does the pre-launch plan differ from a typical brand plan?   78
   What are the key components of a pre-launch brand plan?   79
   How does the need to deliver integrated marketing communications affect the way we
      approach pre-launch planning?   80
   How to approach the development of the pre-launch plan   82
   Frequently asked questions   84

An activity to help you test your skills   85
Definitions of terms used   85
Recommended reading   86

Part II   Planning for an In-line Brand   87

8   Reviewing the Market Size, Value and Competitor Dynamics   89
What is it that we are trying to understand?   89
What are the deliverables from this analysis?   90
What thinking frameworks facilitate this review?   90
How you should approach the review   91
Maximizing the utility of market research   94
Frequently asked questions   96
An activity that you might undertake to help you improve your skill at reviewing the size
    of the market   97
Definitions of terms used   98
Recommended reading   98

9   Reviewing the Brand Situation   99
What is it that we are trying to understand?   99
What is the deliverable?   101
What are the challenges?   101
How to approach the review   101
Maximizing the utility of market research   106
Frequently asked questions   107
An activity that you might undertake to help you improve your skill at reviewing the
    brand situation   108
Definitions of terms used   108
Recommended reading   110

10   Setting New Brand Objectives   111
What is it that we are trying to do?   111
How to set 'new' non-financial objectives   112
Maximizing the utility of market research   114
Frequently asked questions   114
An activity that you might undertake to help you improve your skill at setting non-
    financial objectives   115
Definitions of terms used   116
Recommended reading   116

11   Planning for Implementation   117
The purpose of a brand plan   117
What are the key components of a brand plan?   117
How does the need to deliver integrated marketing communications affect the way you
    approach the design and development of your brand plan?   120
Making your communications work   120
How to approach the development of the brand plan   122

Frequently asked questions   124
An activity to help you test your skills   125
Recommended reading   125

12 REVIEWING THE SALES FORECAST   126
What do we need to understand from the sales forecast?   126
How to approach the 'strategic' forecast   126
How to approach the 'operational' forecast   129
Frequently asked questions   131
An activity to help you test your skills   131
Definitions of terms used   131
Recommended reading   132

13 BUILDING THE BRAND THROUGH EFFECTIVE COMMUNICATION   133
Building brands: the implications   133
How to develop integrated communication   134
Guidelines for effective communication   137
Frequently asked questions   137
An activity that you might undertake to help you improve your skill at reviewing the size
    of the market   141
Definitions of terms used   141
Recommended reading   142

14 MONITORING AND CONTROLLING THE IMPLEMENTATION OF THE BRAND PLAN   143
What is meant by monitoring and control, and why is it necessary?   143
What are the key considerations in developing your approach to monitoring and
    control?   144
Frequently asked questions   145
An activity to help you test your skills   146
Recommended reading   146

CONCLUSION   147
Overcome the challenges   147
Adopt a customer focus – it is an essential ingredient   147
Don't avoid segmenting and targeting   148
Clarify the roles and responsibilities of the central team vs. the local markets   148
Get the whole organization to support the brand   151
Create a structure   153

Index   155

List of Figures

I.1	Generic vs. Branded	3
I.2	Brand Equity Shifts the Demand Curve	5
I.3	A Global Brand Planning Service	6
1.1a	Example Patient: Elderly Patient Severely Impaired with Osteoporosis	12
1.1b	Example Patient: Middle-aged Female at Risk of Osteoporosis	13
1.2	An Example of 'Laddering'	14
2.1a	Patient Flow Diagram for Someone with Persistent Asthma	20
2.1b	Patient Flow Diagram for Someone with PCHF (Previously Had an MI)	20
2.2	Risk Assessment	22
3.1	Example Product Audit	36
3.2	Example Brand Audit	37
3.3	Example of the Equity that Exists for Volvo	37
4.1	Marketing Concepts	44
4.2	Example Strategic Decision Grid	45
4.3	Example SWOT Analysis	45
4.4	Example 'Success Factor' Brainstorm	50
6.1	Future Market Size and Potential	65
6.2	Example Brand Strategy	69
6.3	Hypothetical Brand Guidance for Zofran™	72
7.1	The Marketing Communications Mix	81
7.2	Brand Dynamics Pyramid	83
8.1a	Patient Flow Diagram for Someone with Persistent Asthma	90
8.1b	Patient Flow Diagram for Someone with CHF (Previously Had an MI)	91
8.2	Key Market Drivers and their Impact on the Market Size (Potential and Actual)	93
8.3	Key Market Drivers and their Impact on the Market Size and Market Value	96
8.4	Competitor Market Shares and Growth	96
9.1a	SWOT Before the Strategic Review	100
9.1b	SWOT After the Strategic Review	100
9.2	Example Brand Audit	104
10.1	Brand Dynamics Pyramid	112
11.1	The Marketing Communications Mix	119
12.1	How do CSFs Apply to Building the Brand?	129
12.2	What is the Correlation Between Spend and Sales?	130
13.1	Example of Brand Communication Emphasizing Emotional Benefits	135
13.2	Example of Brand Communication Emphasizing Functional Benefits	135
13.3	Example of Brand Communication Emphasizing What the Brand Stands For	136

13.4	Risperdal (1997)	138
13.5	Seretide (2002)	139
13.6	Zestril (1997)	139
13.7	Assessing Impact of Communication	141
14.1	Questionnaire Design	144

List of Tables

1.1	Example Patient Profiles in the Osteoporosis Market Place	13
1.2	Summary of an Approach to Segmentation in the Osteoporosis Market	15
2.1	Structure for Patient Flow Analysis	23
2.2	Assigning a Value to the Different Market Segments	23
2.3	Guidelines for Identifying an Opportunity	24
2.4	Guidelines for Identifying a Threat	25
2.5	Prioritizing the Key Trends and Critical Uncertainties	25
2.6	Examples of Key Trends and Critical Uncertainties	26
2.7	Example of Key Trends Analysis	27
3.1	Example Behavioural Analysis	34
3.2	Example Competitor Performance Analysis	35
3.3	Guidelines for Identifying a Strength	38
3.4	Guidelines for Identifying a Weakness	38
4.1	Framework for Analysis (Segment 3)	46
4.2	Scoring Scales	47
4.3	Segment Scores (Segment 3)	48
5.1	Future Market Size and Potential	55
5.2	Segment Characteristics	56
5.3	How Competitive is Your Product?	56
5.4	Do We Have the Necessary Capabilities?	57
5.5	What is the Required Level of Investment?	57
5.6	Segment Overall Attractiveness	57
5.7	Example Investment Forecast	58
6.1	Expressing Meaning through Visual and Verbal Clues	71
6.2	Brand Element Choice Criteria	73
6.3	A Checklist For ...	74
8.1	Underlying Trend Forecast	92
8.2	Assigning a Value to the Different Market Segments	94
8.3	Revised Value Forecast	95
9.1	Guidelines for Identifying an Opportunity	102
9.2	Guidelines for Identifying a Threat	103
9.3	Guidelines for Identifying a Strength	105
9.4	Guidelines for Identifying a Weakness	105
10.1	Characteristics of Good Tactical Objectives	113
11.1	Template for Reviewing Last Year's Marketing Plan	123
11.2	Checklist Across Communications	124
12.1	Channel Selection	128
12.2	An Approach to Thinking Through the Forecast	129

13.1	Checklist	136
A (1)	The Responsibilities of Central vs. Local Marketing Team (24–36 months pre-launch)	149
A (2)	The Responsibilities of Central vs. Local Marketing Team (12–18 months pre-launch)	150
A (3)	The Responsibilities of Central vs. Local Marketing Team (Launch)	151
B (1)	A Framework for 'Thinking Globally, Acting Locally'	152
B (2)	Example Slide Content	154

Acknowledgements

To *all* the marketing and senior management executives, too numerous to name individually, that I have had the pleasure of working with since the inception of St Clair Consulting in 1994, I would like to communicate my thanks for the discussions, the ideas exchanged, and specifically the real brand and branding challenges – all of which have helped me refine and strengthen my thinking around brands and branding and how this should be applied within the pharmaceutical industry.

It is important that I single out one person in particular – Kate Holloway (of Virtual Brand Planning) with whom I've worked on many projects over the past four years. Kate's helped stimulate my thinking enormously and I believe that between us, we have defined and evolved the brand planning process to the point that is now embodied in this book.

It is also important that I acknowledge the support from a few key people without whom this book would never have materialized. Firstly, my thanks to Camilla Hallett for the many hours she has put in to creating the diagrams, formatting the text and checking and re-checking for consistency. Also, to my father who read and re-read that text that I had written, providing me with feedback as to what did and did not make sense.

Finally, my thanks go to my 'boys' (Cameron, Robert, George and James) for giving me the time it required to write this book. This book is dedicated to you.

Janice MacLennan

Introduction

Increasingly the pharmaceutical industry recognizes the need to professionalize its marketing skills. Despite this recognition, scant attention is paid to the practice of branding. The objective of this book is to increase understanding of the important issues in brand planning and implementing and evaluating branding strategies.

What is a brand?

To answer this question, we will firstly examine the range of definitions on brands.

I turn to those who are regarded as leading authorities in the branding area.

Kevin Keller in his book *Strategic Brand Management* refers to the American Marketing Association's definition of a brand: 'a brand is a name, term, sign, symbol, or design, or a combination of these intended to identify the goods and services of one seller or group of sellers and to differentiate them from those of competition.'

David Aaker talks about brand equity as 'a set of assets (and liabilities) linked to a brand's name and symbol that adds to (or subtracts from) the value provided by the product or service to a firm and/or that firm's customers.'

Stephen King of WPP Group, London, differentiates between product and brand as follows: 'a product is something that is made in a factory; a brand is something that is bought by a customer. A product can be copied by a competitor; a brand is unique. A product can be quickly outdated; a successful brand is timeless.'

Don Williams, Creative Director and Head of P.I. Global offers this definition: '… you can say its name and people immediately think of imagery that is not just the product … a product evokes a function … a brand evokes emotion.'

However, not one of them refers to the fact that the brand resides in the customer's head – it is not tangible, whereas a product is. And this – the fact that it resides in the customer's head – is to my mind the key point. 'The Brand' can come across as a deceptively simple concept. It is not a singular thing! Rather it comprises a complex vessel of strategic meaning. Successful brands have clear and differentiated positionings and are emotionally relevant. The Volkswagen Beetle is a good example of a successful brand – it came to represent simplicity, freedom of expression and anti-establishment sentiments.

Product brand vs. company brand

It is important to understand that there are two main brand cultures which have converged. There is the brand culture of the West, which has been about product branding (largely shaped by companies such as P&G and Mars). This relies on carving up and segmenting the market. Key words here are targeting and positioning. Then there is the brand culture of the East, which is about company brands such as Sony, Toshiba and Mitsubishi. This relies on building trust based on one name and one name only. The name of the company is perceived to be the best candidate for brand name as it personifies power, continuity and status.

For the pharmaceutical industry, given the frequency with which mergers and acquisitions take place, I believe the emphasis has to be on the product brand. However, it is well worth looking more closely at, and capitalizing on, the company name. My thinking is that the company brand should be used to build trust in 'target' therapeutic areas. The product brand(s) should then be used to differentiate themselves from other products and/or services in this therapeutic area, leveraging the company brand as part of its source of authority.

EXAMPLE

ALLEN AND HANBURY'S IN THE UK (A SUBSIDIARY COMPANY BELONGING TO GLAXOSMITHKLINE) IS RECOGNIZED AS A LEADING RESPIRATORY BRAND. ANY PRODUCT COMING OUT OF THE ALLEN AND HANBURY'S STABLE HAS AN IMMEDIATE ADVANTAGE OVER SIMILAR PRODUCTS BECAUSE OF ITS ASSOCIATION WITH THE ALLEN AND HANBURY'S BRAND.

There has perhaps been too much of a tendency for the brand to hide the company, making it little more than a back office. Let's not forget that in many cases the brand originated because of the know-how of the company. The idea here is that one should create a source of customer-based equity for the product brand, through the company brand.

What is branding?

Branding is considered to be the creation of a bond with your customers through distinctive delivery and in a manner that is consistent with the brand promise. This means breaking down functional barriers and focusing everyone's day-to-day activities on delivering superior performance across key brand triggers. These key brand triggers are recognized as being critical to the success of the brand.

In this industry we often see distinctive delivery (brand names, logos, slogans and advertising images) but often in a manner that is inconsistent with the brand promise. There are products with high levels of name awareness, but with mixed messages associated with them. A new claim, a new formulation, has often ended up as a new message. This is not branding.

Even in companies where today there is branding dialogue, it is rarely focused on brand delivery. The discussion frequently spirals down into a dialogue about the logo, advertising, strapline and promotion, or the discussion remains at too high a level (that is, what the brand is) to have any impact.

In most cases, this lack of a wide-ranging integrated discussion on branding and the implications for each function reflects the lack of experience of branding in the pharmaceutical industry.

Is branding important to the pharmaceutical industry?

There are differences in opinion as to whether branding needs to be practised or not.

- The argument for branding is that it sharpens the uptake curve, and provides protection from products with similar profiles – sustainable differentiation can only come through branding.
- The argument against branding is that in this industry, once the patent has expired, branding offers no protection against the switch to generics.

I hope to convince you that the case for building strong brands is a powerful one in the pharmaceutical industry.

Let's start off with considering the question: if it's important, why has it been ignored? An industry made up primarily of scientists understands the need to create value. However, the industry's formula for creating value has been:

1. investment in R&D in search of innovation
2. patents to protect the innovation
3. studies to demonstrate better patient outcomes than competitor products
4. sales representatives to promote these products
5. marketing departments focused on providing the sales force with promotional support.

There has been limited understanding of how marketing, and branding in particular, can create value. And why should there be?

- Many of the industry marketers are scientists, or have been salespeople. Rational decision-making has been emphasized.
- Companies have done well implementing the above formula.
- Classic marketing textbooks are the basis for learning about marketing, and so the 'product life cycle' has tended to drive the business model. Marketing investment only occurs just before product launch, and how much is invested depends on which stage of the life cycle it is in.

So why consider branding your products?

- Increasingly, therapeutic areas are becoming crowded with different product offerings. Indeed, the global generics market is set to show significant expansion over the next five years (see Figure I.1). As generic competition intensifies, only innovation in branded portfolios will help companies escape this increasing competition and pressure on pricing. *Branding offers the opportunity to differentiate.*

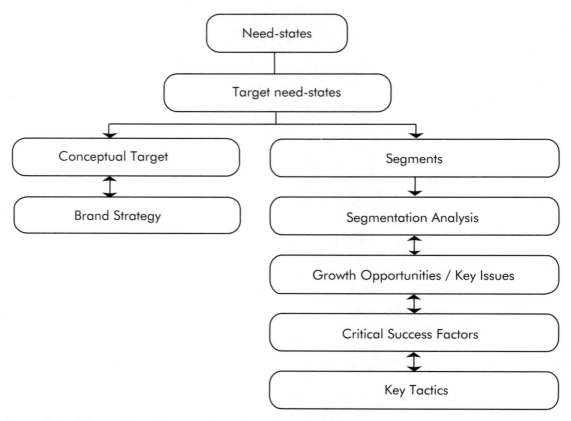

FIGURE I.3   A GLOBAL BRAND PLANNING SERVICE

Adapt this general model to the needs of your business, striving always to achieve the following:

- a well-defined vocabulary
- the same strategic analysis inputs
- the same structure
- the same outputs.

And for now – enjoy the journey!

About This Book

Brand Planning for the Pharmaceutical Industry is split into two parts.

Part One sets out to provide guidance on how to develop a brand plan for a new product. That is, a plan for a product which is either pre-product decision or the plan that is required immediately after this event to provide direction for the clinical trial programme(s). It assumes that a brand strategy needs to be formulated in order to provide direction for the clinical trials and other strategic activities. Given that at this stage in the product's development it is impossible to state with any degree of certainty what can and cannot be claimed, the only certainty you are working with is that of the market and the customer – another argument why 'customer insight' plays such a critical role in the development of this initial thinking around brand strategy and the brand plan.

Part Two, on the other hand, provides guidance for an 'in-line' brand. That is, a brand that is already on the market in one or more of the major markets. It assumes that the brand strategy is defined (or a given) and that the emphasis in planning is on refining the implementation of the strategy rather than formulating it. It also emphasizes the need for understanding the market and the customer. However, the focus is now on the perceptions about your product and competitor products and what this means for how you should move forward, given your understanding of the opportunities and threats in the market.

1

Market Segmentation

In this chapter we will consider:

- What is market segmentation?
- The segmentation approach that is necessary for the purposes of brand planning
- How to segment a market for the purposes of brand planning
- Guidelines for market research
- Frequently asked questions
- An activity that you might undertake to help you improve your skill at inferring segments
- Definitions of terms used
- Recommended reading.

What is market segmentation?

Market segmentation is the starting point if you are considering introducing a new product brand. So what is meant by market segmentation?

Let's start with the term 'segmentation'. **Segmentation** means understanding, and to be able to market effectively, you must understand your consumer and the customers serving the consumer. Ultimately, people with, or at risk of, disease consume the medicines provided by the pharmaceutical industry – this is your consumer. Families, the physician, the payer, the nurse, and other healthcare professionals may influence, or even determine, what the 'consumer' receives. In this book I distinguish the latter from the former (the consumer) by referring to them as customers.

Market segmentation is about grouping your 'potential consumers' in a way that – to the physician – suggests a rationale for a series of different product offerings. It is the process of placing the people who could benefit from your product, either today or at some time in the future, into a group with similar and relevant clinical and emotional needs. The people who are less likely to benefit from your product are grouped into separate segments – the number depending on the extent to which their needs differ. The clinical and emotional needs that are considered are those that might directly or indirectly influence 'product choice'.

The 'need set' for each market segment may be more or less influenced by the patients' actual needs, the payer's needs, and so on. This will vary according to the market situation.

3. Discuss these patient profiles with physicians (or internally if you have a lot of experience in the market). Explore what it is that they are, or might be, trying to achieve/do, given these different 'patients'. Move on to a discussion about the product attributes (or product dimensions) that they believe will be important when deciding what to prescribe for each patient profile. The important thing to remember is that the goal is to have the people you are interviewing name the relevant attributes (you should not produce this list).

4. Now introduce the product profile for your 'new product'. Ascertain whether there is anything about your product that they believe is important and needs to be added to the list of attributes already identified.

5. When you have a satisfactory number of dimensions, you want the respondent to rate the relative importance of each (again given the context of the patient profile). The most important dimensions are then used in the next phase of the interview.

6. Now you need to ask a series of questions. Starting with one of the significant attributes, ask: 'Why is that important to you?' Usually the answer will involve some consequence of the attribute. You then ask the same question again, occasionally rephrasing, for example: 'What does it enable you to do? To achieve?' Persevere with trying to understand the answer to the question – 'And why is that important?' – until the respondent is no longer able to answer the question. Questions such as 'Why is that important?' and 'So what?' are very powerful in this type of investigation

7. Summarize each of the respondent's answers as a ladder (see Figure 1.2). Look for common themes emerging from the research that you have done. Link the themes to the patient characteristics. Use these common themes to formulate market segments (need-states).

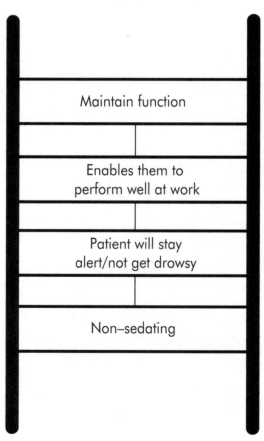

FIGURE 1.2 AN EXAMPLE OF 'LADDERING'

8. For each need-state, you need to end up with a label for the segment, a description of the patient profile and a set of clinical and emotional needs – see Table 1.2. The needs will comprise both clinical and emotional needs. It is only by combining our understanding of the clinical and emotional needs that we develop our customer insight. This insight serves you well in a number of ways – it can later be incorporated into your external analysis and represent an opportunity and/or it can serve as the basis for developing your brand strategy.

9. You then need to decide which need-state to target. This target need-state and the associated patient segments form the context for all further analyses.

TABLE 1.2   SUMMARY OF AN APPROACH TO SEGMENTATION IN THE OSTEOPOROSIS MARKET

Strengthen	Protect	Relieve symptoms
Clinical needs	**Clinical needs**	**Clinical needs**
Maintain bone quality	Minimize bone quantity and quality loss	Speed of relief
Improve bone thickness	Well tolerated	Well tolerated
Improve bone density	Safe	Can be taken as needed
Emotional needs	**Emotional needs**	**Emotional needs**
Patient needs honesty	Patient feels a sense of loss	Patient feels resigned; defeated
Physician feels upbeat, optimistic	Physician is aware of the inevitability of it all	Physician feels sympathetic
Need-state characteristics	**Need-state characteristics**	**Need-state characteristics**
Probably a younger patient' This patient has only just been diagnosed as being at risk of osteoporosis. They may be showing the first signs of the condition	This patient has been diagnosed as having osteoporosis although they may not yet have 'fractured' Pressure is now exerted upon the patient and their family to avoid situations which might lead to the patient having a fracture	In this patient, the condition has progressed to the extent that disablement is the dominant treatment target. The patient is largely dependent on the support of carers
The patient is concerned about the implications of their condition. Allaying fears about the future and providing optimism for the future are primary goals. The chief clinical priority is to intervene quickly to correct the problem	The chief clinical priority is to preserve what bone is left for as long as possible: 'Minimize the risk of the patient fracturing'	Clinical priorities focus on keeping the patient as comfortable as possible

- **Market segmentation:** The process of grouping potential consumers of your product in a way that suggests a rationale for a series of different product offerings. That is, developing need-states.

- **Needs:** The physician's treatment goals.

Recommended reading

Croft, Michael J. (1994) *Marketing for Managers: Market Segmentation*, London: Routledge.
Dibb, S. & Simkin, L. (1996) *The Market Segmentation Workbook: Target Marketing for Marketing Managers*, London: Routledge.
McDonald, M. & Dunbar, I. (1995) *Market Segmentation: A step-by-step approach to creating profitable market segments*, Hampshire: Macmillan Press Ltd.

2

External Analysis – the Starting Point

In this chapter we will consider:

- What is meant by 'external analysis'?
- What are the deliverables from this analysis?
- What are the key ingredients of the external analysis?
- How to approach the external analysis
- Guidelines for market research
- Frequently asked questions
- An activity to help you test your skills
- Definitions of terms used
- Recommended reading.

What is meant by 'external analysis'?

When building a brand plan for a new product, the first question that has to be addressed is: 'Where are we now?' Examining the external and internal situation enables this understanding. The process of studying the external situation in this book is referred to as the external analysis. An external analysis should cover the macro-environment (the different existing environmental forces) and the micro-environment (the segments, customers and competitors). In this chapter I recommend a number of analytical processes that I have found extremely useful to structure my thinking about the external environment. These analytical processes are described in more detail in the sections entitled 'What are the key ingredients of the external analysis?' and 'How to approach the external analysis'.

What are the deliverables from this analysis?

After having completed this analysis you will have an appreciation of the size of each patient segment (sub-group) and the value of each patient segment and what you expect these numbers will be at the end of your planning timeframe.

You will also have an appreciation of the likely profitability of each patient segment and, specifically, the opportunities that exist as well as the threats (or barriers).

What are the key ingredients of the external analysis?

THE PATIENT FLOW ANALYSIS

So what does a patient flow analysis look like? The patient flow may well vary according to the therapeutic area. Essentially, one is interested in identifying the key decision points that affect what happens to the patient from the point at which the condition manifests itself through to the point that they receive drug treatment. Figure 2.1a illustrates a sample patient flow for patients with persistent asthma (a segment of the asthma market). This is contrasted with a patient flow diagram for patients with chronic heart failure and who has also previously suffered from a myocardial infarction (a segment of the CHF market) (see Figure 2.1b).

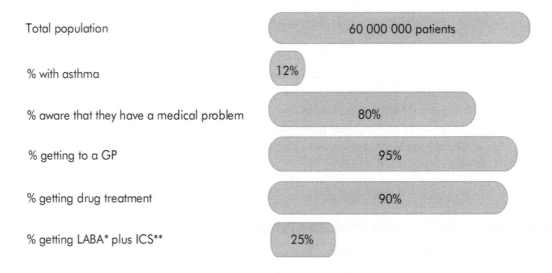

*   LABA (Long acting bronchodilator)
** ICS (inhaled corticosteroid)

FIGURE 2.1A   PATIENT FLOW DIAGRAM FOR SOMEONE WITH PERSISTENT ASTHMA

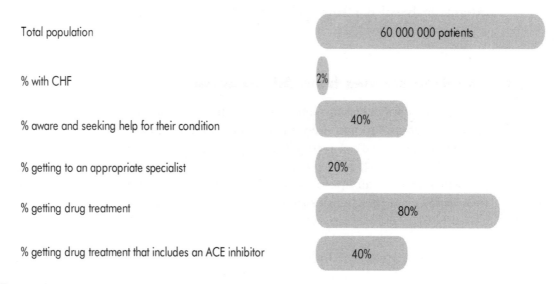

FIGURE 2.1B   PATIENT FLOW DIAGRAM FOR SOMEONE WITH PCHF (PREVIOUSLY HAD AN MI)

If done comprehensively, then for each patient segment associated with the target need-state there will be an understanding of 'what is happening' to the patient, along with the insights as to why this is happening.

COMPETITOR ANALYSIS

Because of the way you are approaching this analysis, when it comes to competition we are interested in identifying the other Rx products that your product will be competing with at the bottom rung of the patient flow. There is a need to understand how they are performing at this decision point, i.e. what share of the patient opportunity do they have and what share of the market value do they have?

Indirect competitors will be managed as threats to the potential if they satisfy an unmet need. They will not be included when trying to 'value the actual market'.

THE KEY TRENDS ANALYSIS

This analysis is necessary to ensure that any future strategy is based on both the shape and the nature of the market today, as well as how this might change in the future. You typically complete a key trends analysis only after you are convinced that you have a good understanding of the market – as it exists today.

The quality of thought, debate and discussion that is put into the interpretation of the future is very important, and makes this analysis worthwhile.

When considering the future there is an awful lot that could be different and probably an equal amount that could be the same. The challenge is to identify those factors that are going to significantly change the shape and/or nature of the future market. The focus is on events which will take place and that are independent of your own strategy.

With the future there are no facts. At best you have a high degree of certainty (a) that an event will take place and (b) about the implication of that event on each market segment. Events that honour these principles are referred to as key trends. In some cases it is likely that the event itself or the implication of the event is surrounded by a degree of uncertainty – these events will be referred to as critical uncertainties.

The business strategy is formulated in the context of these key trends and critical uncertainties, and the opportunities and threats that these key trends and critical uncertainties present.

- The events where the outcome is uncertain but the potential impact is significant (critical uncertainties) can be used to test the viability of a proposed strategy. That is, are the returns still worthwhile if one or more of these outcomes should happen? This is referred to as risk assessment (see Figure 2.2).
- A different way that the critical uncertainties are used is in considering different market scenarios. The strategy can be formulated given the context of different market scenarios. That is, the critical uncertainties are used to formulate a scenario, which then provides the context within which the strategy is formulated.

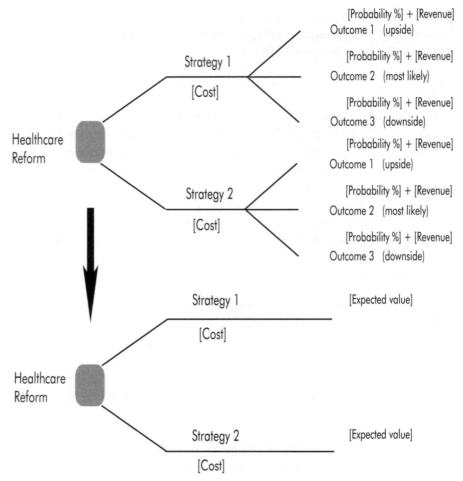

FIGURE 2.2   RISK ASSESSMENT

How to approach the external analysis

You should structure your external analysis around the relevant patient segments and the patient flow.

1. Develop a structure for the patient flow. This structure needs to be one that can be applied to each market segment. This requires that you understand the significant decision areas that influence what happens to the patient, from the point at which the condition manifests itself to the point at which the patient receives treatment.

2. Structure your patient flow like an epidemiology-based forecasting model. You might find the following questions helpful:
   - Are people aware that they have a problem?
   - Do they get to a physician?
   - Is their condition easy to recognize?
   - Do they get medication?
   - Do they get the 'appropriate' medication?

3. The first challenge is to identify where in the process patients are being 'lost' (i.e. is there potential for market expansion and, if so, where is this potential and how big is it?) Record your conclusions. Note that the way the majority of people will do this is by using the

TABLE 2.1 STRUCTURE FOR PATIENT FLOW ANALYSIS

Decision area	% retention	Actual numbers	Insights
% aware they have a problem			
% getting to a PCP			
% with their condition recognized			
% attaining an 'appropriate medication'			

concept of retention – that is, how many people from the 'decision phase' above reach the next decision phase. Record this as a percentage (see Table 2.1).

4. Now identify whom you are competing with for that prescription at the 'final decision phase'. Who are the relevant competitors? How many should be included? Which ones should be considered? You're best answering these questions by talking to customers.
   - Give a group of customers a description of the patient segments. Ask them which products they most often use in each patient segment.
   - A second group of customers can be given a list of products and asked how likely they are to use the product in each of the patient segments.
   - Allocate the products to the patient segments based on their perceived appropriateness for each market segment.

5. Once you have listed whom you are competing with in each patient segment, gather the sales data for these products. Where the product is used in more than one segment, this data needs to be apportioned to the relevant segments in order for you to be able to determine a value for each market segment (see Table 2.2).

6. The next challenge is getting to the insights. Examine each decision point and ask yourself:
   - 'Are there insights about what is going on at this decision point which represent openings to the potential? And if so, what are they?' These will be interpreted as opportunities; and
   - 'Do we have any insight about what is going on at this decision point that could be regarded as barriers to the potential? And if so, what are they?' These will be interpreted as threats.

TABLE 2.2 ASSIGNING A VALUE TO THE DIFFERENT PATIENT SEGMENTS

List of brands [total value]	Segment 1	Segment 2	Segment 3
Brand A [$100m]	$80m	$10m	$10m
Brand B [$500m]	—	$500	—
Brand C [$800m]	—	$700	$100m
Brand D [$900m]	$100m	$200m	$600m

Note: the fact that very few people (or rather a small percentage of people) reach a decision point is not necessarily indicative of barriers – this could be because of unmet need (and therefore an opportunity).

EXAMPLE

PRE-VIAGRA, THE NUMBER OF PEOPLE RECEIVING AN RX TREATMENT FOR ERECTILE DYSFUNCTION MAY HAVE BEEN LOW. THIS WAS BECAUSE OF THE UNMET PATIENT NEED OF 'AN ACCEPTABLE SOLUTION', WHICH WAS ONE OF THE OPPORTUNITIES.

These opportunities and threats will be inferred from (and should be supported by) market research that you have undertaken. Note that the insight into the opportunities and threats that exist in relation to the key decision points will not result from one market research study but rather be built up over time, over several years.

7. Summarize, for each segment, your understanding of what is happening (i.e. in terms of patient numbers, or market behaviour) and why what is happening is happening (market knowledge and insight).

8. Interpret the insight into opportunities and threats. The opportunities and threats will vary by segment and will be describing the market situation as it exists today. Tables 2.3 and 2.4 show some guidelines for the classification of opportunities and threats.

9. Now develop a list of future events. In the first instance include anything and everything that springs to mind as being something that could impact the market within the defined planning timeframe (typically three to five years in a local operating company and five-plus years for a central product strategy team).

TABLE 2.3   GUIDELINES FOR IDENTIFYING AN OPPORTUNITY

An opportunity is	An opportunity is not
… anything that is outside your direct control and provides a 'way into accessing the market potential'	… something within your control
… something which you and/or your competitors can take advantage of to penetrate the market	… something that is only available to you
… something that exists or may emerge in the near future	… something that you have to create or do

Table 2.4   Guidelines for Identifying a Threat

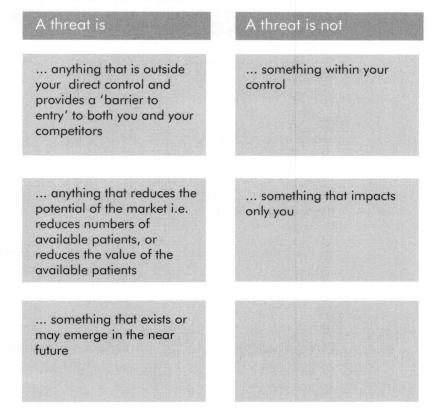

A threat is	A threat is not
... anything that is outside your direct control and provides a 'barrier to entry' to both you and your competitors	... something within your control
... anything that reduces the potential of the market i.e. reduces numbers of available patients, or reduces the value of the available patients	... something that impacts only you
... something that exists or may emerge in the near future	

10. Evaluate these events in terms of: (a) their likelihood of happening, and (b) the impact that they might have on the market (either positive or negative), working on the assumption that they will happen (see Table 2.5). The shortlist that you are left with will comprise a mixture of key trends and critical uncertainties (see Table 2.6).
   - A '**key trend**' is an event that you feel fairly certain will happen in the future and whose market impact is significant.
   - A '**critical uncertainty**' is an event that may happen. If it does happen, it will have a significant impact on one or more of the patient segments. Alternatively, it could include an event that you are certain will happen – but the uncertainty is around how it might impact the market and specifically the different patient segments.

Table 2.5   Prioritizing the Key Trends and Critical Uncertainties

Event	Probability	Impact	Key trend	Critical uncertainty
Event one	High	High	✓	☒
Event two	Medium	High	☒	✓
Event three	Medium	Medium	☒	☒
Event four, etc.	Low	Medium	☒	☒

TABLE 2.6   EXAMPLES OF KEY TRENDS AND CRITICAL UNCERTAINTIES

Key trends	Critical uncertainties
Competitive technological breakthroughs (e.g. pulmonary insulin)	Regulatory delay of new products
New product launches	Price wars
Introduction of disease treatment guidelines	Reduction of trade barriers
Higher disease awareness	Patients becoming more knowledgeable about their disease and treatment options
Patient expiration	Discovery of new diagnostic
Increased regulation, etc.	

11. Once you have a shortlist of key trends and critical uncertainties that you have decided to incorporate into your thinking about the future, you need to consider the impact that these events might have on each patient segment.

    In the first instance you need to decide whether the trend is likely to affect the market size (i.e. number of patients or patient opportunities), the average treatment value of any one patient, or help one or more of the brands compete for market share.

12. Where you have an event that will impact the market size (i.e. of patients or of patient opportunities), decide at which point in the patient flow the primary impact will occur.

13. If you are using the patient flow data to inform your forecast then you should also decide when the market might feel the impact and by what percentage it is likely to grow (or decline).

14. For all key trends and uncertainties – interpret as an opportunity, a threat, or as having no impact. Repeat for each patient segment. Make a note of why you have interpreted it this way. You will be surprised how often you forget why you or your team took a certain view about the future (see Table 2.7).

15. Repeat for each patient segment.

TABLE 2.7 EXAMPLE OF KEY TRENDS ANALYSIS

Key trends	... with the potential to affect the level of investment required	... with the potential to affect segment value	... with the potential to affect segment size
1.		Opportunity (increases customer's willingness to pay)	
2.	No impact		
3.			Potential threat (reduces numbers attaining appropriate medication)
Critical uncertainties			
1.			Opportunity (increases numbers seeking treatment)
2.	Potential threat (increases the need for additional manpower)		

EXAMPLE

CONSIDER THE INTRODUCTION OF ANOTHER AGENT FOR THE TREATMENT OF OSTEOPOROSIS. IT COULD MEAN THAT MORE WOMEN AT RISK OF OSTEOPOROSIS SEEK TREATMENT BECAUSE THERE IS A GREATER LEVEL OF AWARENESS OF 'WHO IS AT RISK'. ALL PLAYERS IN THIS MARKET WOULD REGARD THIS AS A FUTURE OPPORTUNITY. BECAUSE A SIGNIFICANT NUMBER OF PEOPLE AT RISK OF OSTE-OPOROSIS, AND EVEN WITH OSTEOPOROSIS, DO NOT CONSULT THEIR DOCTOR, THIS EVENT COULD WELL IMPACT ALL SEGMENTS EQUALLY.

NOW CONSIDER THE INTRODUCTION OF YET ANOTHER COMMUNITY ANTIBIOTIC BY ONE OF THE TOP TEN PHARMACEUTICAL COM-PANIES. ASSUME THIS COMPANY HAD A NUMBER OF PRODUCTS GOING OFF PATENT AND THAT THIS WAS THE ONLY NEW PRODUCT IT WAS INTRODUCING FOR THE NEXT FEW YEARS. THIS WOULD BE INTERPRETED AS A SIGNIFICANT THREAT TO ANY SEGMENTS INVOLVING PATIENTS WITH COMMUNITY INFECTION BECAUSE IT WOULD BE ASSUMED THAT THE COMPANY'S EXISTING RESOURCES (FOR EXAMPLE, SALES FORCE, MARKETING EXPENDITURE ETC.) MIGHT BE APPLIED TO ENSURE THE FAST UPTAKE OF THIS NEW ANTIBIOTIC. TO DEFEND THEIR SHARE WILL REQUIRE AN INCREASE IN INVESTMENT BY THE OTHER PLAYERS – THIS IS WHY IT IS A THREAT. IT WOULD BE UNLIKELY TO IMPACT SEGMENTS INVOLVING HOSPITALIZED PATIENTS.

16. Add these opportunities and threats to the opportunities and threats that you have already described for each market segment. You have now completed your external analysis. You are now able to explain the current and predicted future value and size of each segment, and the environment that you will be competing in, in each segment (as summarized by the opportunities and threats).

Guidelines for market research

1. An important thing to remember is that an insight is only as good as its interpretation. Research that you undertake probably won't produce a clear, single message. Much of what you learn will be open to interpretation, and many different interpretations may be legitimate. Your challenge is to resist the 'eureka' impulse of latching on to one message and ignoring other, possibly contradictory, bits of information. It is important to keep an open mind and consider the information from many different viewpoints to try to understand the full spectrum of what you have heard or seen. The more open you are, the better you will be at making connections between your observations and your business.

2. The goal of understanding the customer is fundamental. Understanding is an active process. This does not mean just using 'market research' as an information source. It is necessary to avoid the trap of simply assuming that understanding increases with the amount of data available. Our industry is particularly guilty – if I may say so – of trying to achieve understanding through data. Understanding is not just a matter of data. It is first and foremost a matter of explanation. To understand something is to explain how it happens. This can involve making a prediction about what will happen. But explanation is more than prediction.

   In looking for explanations, the important thing to realize is that the explanation is never in the data but always separate from data. The only way to predict is to have an explanation. Predicting from data alone is not logically justified.

   So where do explanations come from? If not from data, where else? Explanations come from creativity. Explanation is the creative act of figuring out what is going on in the market. Such creativity may be inspired by data, looking at patterns of data until one gets an idea of what is going on. Or it may follow from other creative impulses, including experience and intuition. The crucial thing is to have an explanation.

   So what is the role of data? It is to increase your confidence in the explanation you hold or to challenge the explanation you hold and encourage you to look for a better one. Data is the most powerful way of critiquing an explanation.

   Above all, understanding is hardest to achieve. It involves trying to explain why people do what they do. It is difficult enough to explain anything, but explaining people's behaviour is harder still. What is really important is one's ability and willingness to confront explanations without data, so that data then poses a severe test of the explanation. If an explanation survives testing, it is accepted but not proven. If an explanation fails, we must create a better explanation and test it so that explanations can evolve over time. This approach should produce not just marketing research, but knowledge.

Frequently asked questions

- **What is an insight?** An insight is an understanding of the market that 'wows' you. It is an understanding that suddenly makes sense of the market behaviour. It often relates to a better understanding of the attitudes and beliefs that are driving the behaviour.
- **How do I know whether the insight represents an opportunity or a threat?** Refer to the guidelines provided earlier in this chapter for what is an opportunity and what is a threat. Basically, if you feel you need to overcome something, change something about the external environment, or defend yourself from something, it is likely to be a threat.

- **Is correct classification of opportunities and threats important?** In my view it is. Investment in opportunities results in market share gains. Investment in threats might mean market development (which could result in increased sales but maintaining share), or market expansion (again an increase in sales without necessarily impacting your market share).

  It is especially important that each external factor is recorded as either an opportunity or a threat, rather than as a strength or a weakness. Unless it is something you particularly want to invest in, it may not be worth spending too much time debating on which side of the vertical line the external factors end up. That is to say, don't spend unnecessary energy debating whether it is an opportunity or a threat.

- **Why are we concerned about whether something is a future trend or already in existence?** It is really very important to develop your understanding of the patient segments as they are today before you start considering how these might change in the future. This is important because you need to overlay any view about the future on to the reality of today. You cannot consider future changes in isolation. Also, when you do your market forecast, typically you would project the underlying historical trend and only then overlay your assumptions about the events that then lead to an adjustment of this underlying trend.

- **Why is it important to think through the implications for each patient segment?** When planning for new products you are trying to understand the 'future commercial attractiveness' of each patient segment, in terms of patient numbers, value and future growth (or possible decline). You are also trying to understand the 'feasibility' of realizing the potential for your product in each patient segment. If you do not think through the implications of future events at a segment level, you can miss some of the insights that are there to be discovered.

An activity to help you test your skills

Refer back to an old plan that you have written or a plan that exists on the system that has been written by a colleague. Find the page summarizing the SWOT analysis. Focus on the OT part of the SWOT. Is there any evidence of the author of the plan recognizing that the opportunities and threats may be different in different parts of the market? How is this described? How might you have done this differently?

Ask yourself the following questions: Would I have interpreted any of these items differently? Is everything that is described as an opportunity a 'true opportunity'? Amend the summary of opportunities. Ask yourself whether the opportunity would have emerged from the patient flow analysis or key trends analysis.

For those opportunities that emerge as a result of the key trends analysis, could they impact the future market size? If yes, look to see whether the forecast for the future market has been adjusted in light of the key trend (i.e. look for consistency in thinking).

Now move across to the threats. Evaluate the threats in the same way – are they all items that you would have described as threats?

Definitions of terms used

- **Competition:** This includes any company which provides or will be in a position to offer a product/service or solution that meets the customers' needs.
- **Competitor analysis:** The determination for each patient segment of the relative strengths and weaknesses of:
  — the company's capability to address opportunities and threats
  — the products' ability to satisfy patients' therapeutic needs vs. relevant competitor products.
- **Critical uncertainties:** Those trends and/or changes whose impact on the future shape or nature of the market is thought to be 'high,' but where the likelihood of them happening is either 'low' or 'medium'.
- **Decision phases:** The key steps that determine what happens to the patient: whether they get into the healthcare system, and what happens to them once they are in the system.
- **Future market assessment:** The process for systematically appraising the external environment and, in so doing, anticipating and planning for changes which (it is thought) will have a significant impact on the market. This will contain a set of assumptions about trends and how they will impact on the future. The acronym 'PESTLE' guides the analysis of potential changes that may affect the overall context in which a market exists:
  — Political
  — Environmental
  — Social/cultural
  — Technical/technological limitations
  — Legal/government regulation
  — Economic.
  The '5 Forces' (a.k.a. The Porter Model) guides the analysis of potential changes that may occur within a market:
  — threat of new entrants
  — threat of substitutes
  — bargaining power of customers
  — bargaining power of suppliers
  — leverage of complementers.
- **Insight:** Describes the key reason(s) underpinning the market behaviour.
- **Key trends:** Those trends and/or changes whose impact on the future shape or nature of the market is thought to be high, and where the likelihood of them happening is also high.
- **Market analysis:** The market analysis develops your understanding of the opportunities and threats that exist in the market today. Its purpose is to establish the actual size of each market segment, the potential size of each market segment and the opportunities and barriers that exist within both the potential and actual markets.
- **Market research:** Information used to identify and define marketing opportunities and challenges; generate and refine marketing actions; monitor marketing performance; and improve the understanding of marketing as a process.
- **Market value:** The total sales value of competing products in a given market.
- **Market volume:** The total number of 'available' patients or patient opportunities in a given market.

- **Opportunity:** A condition of the environment that makes the realization of potential more likely. Opportunities will include trends that could, potentially, have a positive effect on the market because they will increase or facilitate access to the market. Opportunity is independent of whether or not the company has the capabilities to capture/realize it.
- **Patient flow:** This is a thinking framework used to assess the market to determine the strategic issues which are resulting in a gap between the 'true' patient potential and the actual size of the market.
- **Potential:** The amount of business that might be realized in the market if the total population who could benefit from the therapeutic approach had access to the treatment.
- **Threat:** A condition in the environment that is unattractive because it could have a damaging effect on the market. It could be either reducing market potential or closing the windows of opportunity – regardless of the company's capabilities to manage the condition.
- **Trends:** Identified or forecast patterns of change over time.

Recommended reading

Dogramatzis, Dimitris (2001) *Pharmaceutical Marketing: A practical guide*, Denver, Colorado: IHS Health Group.

Fifield, P. (1999) *Marketing Strategy. Second Edition*, Oxford: Butterworth-Heinemann.

Kotler, P. (1988) *Marketing Management: Analysis, Planning, Implementation and Control* (6th edition), New Jersey, USA: Prentice-Hall International.

3

The Internal Analysis – the Next Step

In this chapter we will consider:

- What is the internal analysis?
- What are the deliverables from this analysis?
- What are the key ingredients of this analysis?
- How to approach the internal analysis
- Guidelines for market research
- Frequently asked questions
- An activity to help you test your skills
- Definitions of terms used
- Recommended reading.

What is the internal analysis?

The sure road to product failure is introducing or managing a product that has no perceptible and meaningful point of difference vs. current product offerings. 'Me-tooism' is the disease that afflicts a majority of products. This is why undertaking an internal analysis is so important. It requires you to look critically at both your company and your product, but this critical appraisal takes place in the context of how well you satisfy the segment requirements *and* how well you do this vs. the relevant competition.

What are the deliverables from this analysis?

On completing your internal analysis, you should be able to:

1. develop and/or refine your target product profile (TPP), because you now have a view of:
   (a) the 'musts' for the end points in the clinical trials – based on the needs that are already satisfied in the market
   (b) the end points that might neutralize the competitors' strengths – based on an understanding of what they are perceived to be good at
   (c) the end points that might offer the opportunity for differentiation – based on an understanding of the unmet needs and/or dissatisfaction that exists in the market
2. determine your communications strategy because of your understanding of which associations already exist in thought leaders' heads that need to be managed
3. identify which capabilities you might need as an organization to develop or maintain (nurture) in order to build your brand.

What are the key ingredients of this analysis?

- **The product audit:** This analysis develops your understanding of where the unmet needs and dissatisfactions in this market are. It informs the development and refinement of the 'target product profile'.
- **The brand audit:** This analysis develops your understanding of what the product attributes need to be to make you competitive. It informs the development and refinement of your product position. It also helps you decide which capabilities are needed to maximize the successful commercialization of your brand. It will inform your decision about which piece of the market (i.e. which patient segments) you might go after and, within those segments, which opportunities you should focus on.

How to approach the internal analysis

1. Before you can analyse your competitive position, you need to complete a behavioural analysis (see Table 3.1) of the identified competitors in their respective market segments. You need to understand how each player behaves in the market place, how they have launched their products, how they have responded to the strategies of new entrants, what their response was towards new government regulations, how they have priced and promoted their new product introductions, to what extent they have managed the creation of brands, and so on.

2. You also want a detailed study of the competitors' performance over time – ideally no less than three years, and probably not more than five years into the past. This includes looking at their patient share, value share, unit and cash sales, and growth. You'll probably not be able to get this data at a segment level, yet this is the level at which we need to understand it. However, earlier in your research process, you undertook research that helped you identify which competitors were prescribed in which segments and to what extent. Use this information to apportion the sales data for each brand across the segments. If you estimate the average cost per patient treated per annum, you will be able to approximate each competitor's share of a segment (see Table 3.2).

3. Use this information to formulate your opinion about the competitive situation. Are there gaps? In which patient segments? Do these gaps represent an opportunity for you to attain competitive advantage?

4. Having completed this behavioural and competitor performance analysis (invariably through secondary data sources), you need to undertake primary market research to understand the physicians' perceptions of how well the different products satisfy the needs in each segment. Also, you need this piece of research to help you understand which attributes positively or negatively differentiate one product from another and in which segments, and which attributes are perceived as being common to the majority of products and therefore not differentiating.

5. On receipt of the research findings and conclusions, you should analyse the data that you have as follows:
   - for each segment – list the segment needs in order of priority
   - map, using the research scale (to illustrate I will use a five-point scale), how well each of these needs is satisfied by each of the competing products
   - identify the gaps, i.e. where there are needs unmet or where there is still some dissatisfaction

TABLE 3.1   EXAMPLE BEHAVIOURAL ANALYSIS

Behaviour	Competitor 1	Competitor 2	Competitor 3
Therapeutic category specialization			
Product launch pattern (frequency, success)			
Resourcing for new product launches			
Product life cycle management			
Globalization			
Innovation			
Integration			
Branding			
Pricing			
Product quality			
Services offered			
Competitor responsiveness			
Restructuring			
Reorganization			
Public relations activity			
Push and pull strategies			
Sales force organization			

- summarize your conclusions under the heading 'unmet need'
- repeat for each patient segment.

Figure 3.1 illustrates this analytical approach.

This is typically referred to as the product audit – we now know what the market believes.

6. Now you need to understand why your customers believe what they believe – this is the brand audit. Tease out which attributes positively and/or negatively differentiate the products from each other, and whether these vary at all by segment. Anything that positively differentiates one product from another should be classified as an asset for the product. Anything that negatively differentiates one product from another should be classified as a liability for the product. Those attributes that are assumed to be common to all products should be classified as points of parity. Are there any attributes which could

TABLE 3.2   EXAMPLE COMPETITOR PERFORMANCE ANALYSIS

Brand name / company name	Sales volume	Growth	Market share	Profitability	Quality	Service	Customer satisfaction	Image	Product innovation	Service innovation
1.										
2.										
3.										
4.										
5.										
6.										
7.										

Segment description

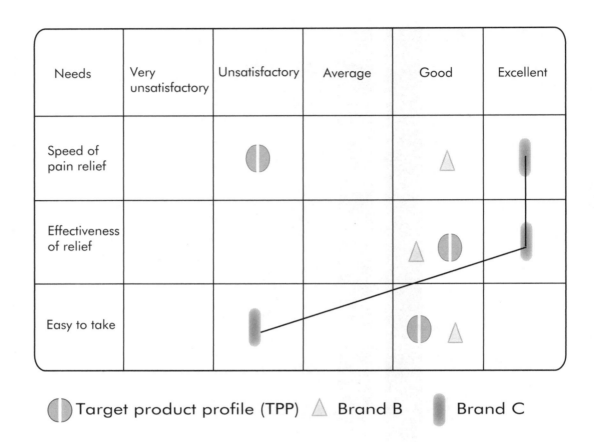

Needs	Very unsatisfactory	Unsatisfactory	Average	Good	Excellent
Speed of pain relief		TPP		Brand B	Brand C
Effectiveness of relief				Brand B, TPP	Brand C
Easy to take		Brand C		TPP	Brand B

◖ Target product profile (TPP)   △ Brand B   ▮ Brand C

FIGURE 3.1   EXAMPLE PRODUCT AUDIT

potentially be associated with your product (or TPP) – both good and bad, which doctors did not mention as being meaningful or relevant to them? List them as potential drivers (if positive) or potential liabilities (if negative). Figure 3.2 illustrates how you might approach this.

7. Interpret your research findings carefully. Prescribing decisions are not always based on the rational criteria customers offer in focus groups and research. Among competitive products, there is often very little difference in quality and product performance. The understanding of the attributes that are associated with this perceived 'need satisfaction' helps us understand the brand equity that exists for each competitor (see the Volvo example in Figure 3.3).

8. Understanding how/why the attribute associations have been formed is essential when planning for a new product. Refer back to the behavioural and competitor performance analysis – what did you learn? What are the factors over and above the product attributes that are working in your favour (add these to the list of assets)? What are the factors that could work in your favour but currently are not (add these to the list of potential drivers)? What are the factors that are working against you (add these to the list of liabilities)? What are the factors that could work against you (add these to the list of potential liabilities)?

9. Now summarize your position. Where you have something listed as an asset, interpret this as a strength and make a note that this is a source of competitive differentiation. Where you have something listed as a liability, interpret this as a weakness. Where you have something described as a potential driver, then also interpret this as a strength and make

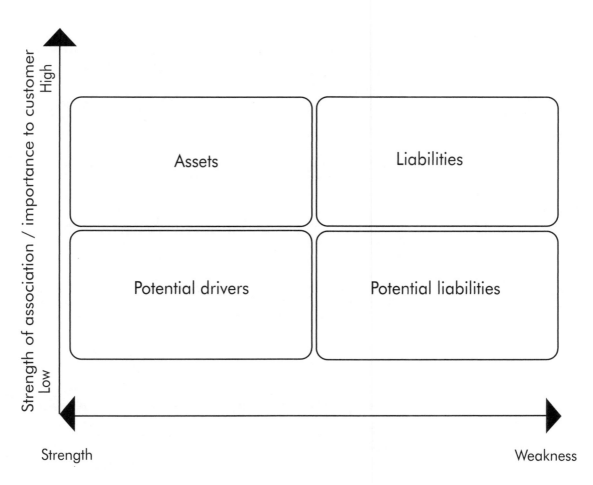

FIGURE 3.2 EXAMPLE BRAND AUDIT

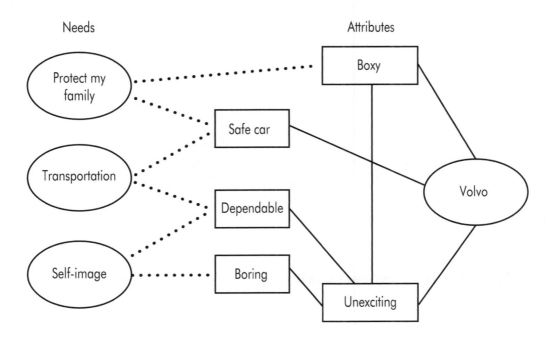

FIGURE 3.3 EXAMPLE OF THE EQUITY THAT EXISTS FOR VOLVO. ADAPTED FROM THE BRAND VALUE MAP, *Kellog on Marketing*

TABLE 3.3   GUIDELINES FOR IDENTIFYING A STRENGTH

A strength is	A strength is not
... something in your control	... something outside your control
... something which provides you with a source of competitive advantage	... something that is equally available to others
... something that is relevant, i.e. it must have market application	... something that you have but which has no obvious market relevance
... something which is a success, a source of brand equity; if it is a source of brand equity, it is an asset	... a description of what you have to do

TABLE 3.4   GUIDELINES FOR IDENTIFYING A WEAKNESS

A weakness is	A weakness is not
... something in your control that is not currently working for you but has relevance	... something outside your control
... a liability – it puts you at a competitive disadvantage	... an asset
... a current state	... not a future state

a note that this represents an opportunity for competitive differentiation. Tables 3.3 and 3.4 show some guidelines for the classification of strengths and weaknesses.

10 When you have completed your internal analysis you will have summarized your understanding of the unmet medical need, and highlighted the opportunities for competitive differentiation. As a result of this analysis you will be able to infer the opportunities that exist for competitive differentiation.

Guidelines for market research

When gathering information to complete your product audit and/or brand audit, here are some thoughts:

- Although direct approaches towards learning perceptions can be useful, often it is worthwhile to consider more indirect methods – even some that might appear a bit offbeat. The indirect approaches often are motivated by the assumption that the people we want to research may be either unwilling or unable to reveal feelings, thoughts and attitudes when asked questions. People may be unwilling because they feel such information is embarrassing or private. Alternatively, they may simply be unable to provide the information as to why certain products are prescribed because they don't know the real reason. Projective research techniques address both these problems, in part by allowing the respondent to project themself into a context which bypasses the inhibitions or limitations of more direct questioning.

- It really is quite important to use indirect approaches to help you understand what the competitor brands mean to the customer(s). This research should be replicated through time and in the context of the different market segments. It is inexcusable to be guessing at people's perceptions of the different brands.

- A more direct way to measure associations is to scale the brands upon a set of dimensions. Scaling approaches are more objective and reliable than qualitative approaches. They can be based on a representative sample of customers and uncover the incidence of associations and the relationship among them. In this way they can be quantified.

- Of concern in any one of these studies is identifying the most important perceptual dimensions. One way of obtaining this information is by asking respondents how important each attribute or benefit is to their choice of brands. The problem here is that often people state everything as being important. A second approach is identifying which attributes discriminate between prescribers and non-prescribers. A third way is asking trade-off questions. The latter technique provides a sensitive measure of dimension importance to a customer. Note that perceptual measurement needs to be done with respect to a specified segment and within the context of a competitive set of brands.

- Another consideration is whether the perceptual dimensions discriminate between brands. If an attribute really discriminates, it might be worth retaining, even though it does not seem important according to other measures (it will be classified as a potential driver or a potential liability). Conversely, if an attribute or benefit patently appears to be important but does not discriminate between brands, then it may be of only marginal usefulness (it will be classified as a point of parity).

  Finally, you should not only be interested in the associations with each of the brands, and the position of the brand on the perceptual dimensions, but also in:
  — the strength of the association, and
  — the clarity of the image, i.e. do customers agree upon the associations with a brand?
  Brands with more clarity around their image and with strong associations will prove to be tough competitors.

- Behavioural analysis of competitors uses historically related data regarding their distinct behaviours and reactions in the market place. This has limitations, particularly if that company has recently acquired a new CEO or if there have been changes to the senior management team. In these circumstances, past behaviour is no longer a predictor of their likely future strategy. However, provided you know where the new CEO or management have come from, you could always study that company's behaviour and try to infer conclusions.

- Performance analysis utilizes long-term historical data about the competitor. Usually, data on the past three to five years. Performance measurements can be expressed in absolute terms or correlated with the industry's performance. This is a critical step because together with the behavioural analysis it provides insights into the relationship between competitors' behaviour and strategy and results.

Frequently asked questions

- **When you're planning for new products how might you use this analysis to help you determine your 'target product profile'?** You can, but you will first need to have decided which market segment (need-state and associated patient segments) you want to target. Assuming you have done this, plot your customers' perception of how well the competitor products satisfy the needs in each patient segment. Identify which attributes are most strongly associated with the competitor products and establish whether these represent assets (i.e. strongly associated and differentiating to the competitor, meaningful to the customer and perceived to be positive), liabilities (as above, except perceived to detract from prescribing) or points of parity (perceived by the customer that most products deliver these).

  The points of parity by definition become 'must haves'. I also argue that you need to select at least one point of difference as a 'must have' to avoid ending up with a 'me-too'. Are there liabilities associated with competitor products that could offer the potential for differentiation? Are there assets that the competitors have that you could neutralize?

  Most target product profiles will contain 'must haves' – these provide the framework for go/no-go decisions before the product gets taken into clincial trials. Then there is typically a list of 'nice to haves'. The 'nice to haves' don't form the basis of go/no-go decisions but very often do provide the basis for differentiation and/or changing the market paradigm. Use your insight into unmet need, perceived dissatisfaction and the associations to work up a target product profile. Focus only on the patient segments that you want to compete in.

- **When the product is in the early stages of development, and accepting that this analysis needs to be based on physician perception – how do we manage this given that our product is not yet on the market?** You'll probably have a number of physicians involved in its development either directly (e.g. participating in the clinical trials) or indirectly (opinion leader panels). Consult these physicians for a perspective about how well they perceive your product will satisfy the requirements.

- **How do you distinguish between a need and an attribute?** A number of parameters can satisfy a need whereas with an attribute you either have it or you do not have it. Let me illustrate this by example. Saying that there is a need for no drug-drug interactions is incorrect. Your product either interacts with other medications or does not. The need is likely to be something like 'Does not inconvenience the patient'.

An activity to help you test your skills

Refer back to an old plan that you have written or a plan that exists on the system that has been written by a colleague. Find the page summarizing the SWOT analysis. Focus on the SW part of the SWOT. Ask yourself these questions:

1. Is there any evidence of the author of the plan recognizing that the strengths and weaknesses may be different in different parts of the market? How is this described? How might I have done this differently?

2. Would I have interpreted any of these items differently?

3. Is everything that is described as a strength something that is relevant (or important) to the market and something that we're better at than the competition? Amend the summary of strengths.

4. Now move across to the weaknesses. Evaluate them in the same way.

5. Now look to see whether the historic market share performance makes sense given this competitive position, i.e. are those companies that are particularly strong the ones that have succeeded in gaining market share at the expense of their weaker competitors? (You're looking for consistency in thinking here.)

Definitions of terms used

- **Assets:** These are attributes unique to the brand and perceived as brand strengths. They build equity. Some assets may be neutralized by competitor activity over time – and therefore would be considered to be 'vulnerable' assets.

- **Attitudes:** How people regard (feel and/or think about) something. Attitudes are more changeable than beliefs.

- **Beliefs:** What people think to be true or not. While beliefs may be more difficult to change than attitudes, beliefs are easier to change than needs, values or motivators.

- **Brand:** The perceptual entity that resides in the mind of the customer and that relates to a product or service.

- **Brand association:** The characteristics of the brand that the customer and/or consumer recall. They can be characteristics that are either liked or disliked.

- **Liabilities:** These are attributes unique to the brand that detract from the brand equity, brand weaknesses.

- **Points of parity:** These attributes of the brand are valued by the customer but are not unique to the brand; as a result, they do not differentiate the brand from others.

- **Potential drivers:** These are attributes that are unique to a brand but are not currently valued or associated with the brand by the customer.

- **Product audit:** An understanding of the product-related strengths and weaknesses in light of the 'needs', and how well these needs are perceived to be satisfied by the competition.

- **Product profile:** A section of a marketing plan describes what the product profile is or is predicted to be. It should contain information on:
  - class of drug, formulation
  - dosage
  - product features (e.g. half-life, drug interactions)
  - formulations
  - the patent situation.

- **Strength:** Factors within the company/team's control that are required to capture opportunities and/or manage threats. These are both strong and stronger than relevant competitors'.

- **Success factors:** The functions, abilities, power and characteristics of the organization that have created the perception that exists about the brand in the market place.

Recommended reading

Aaker, David A. (1991) *Managing Brand Equity*, USA: MacMillan Inc.

Aaker, David A. (1996) *Building Strong Brands*, New York, USA: The Free Press.

Aaker, David A. (2000) *Brand Leadership*, New York, USA: The Free Press.

Blackett, T. and Robins, D. (2001) *Brand Medicine: The role of Branding in the Pharmaceutical Industry*, Hampshire: Palgrave Publishers Ltd.

Dogramatzis, Dimitris (2001) *Pharmaceutical Marketing: A Practical Guide*, Denver, Colorado: IHS Health Group.

Iacobucci, D. (2001) *Kellog on Marketing*, Canada: John Wiley & Sons.

Keller, Kevin L. (1998) *Strategic Brand Management. Building, Measuring, and Managing Brand Equity*, New Jersey, USA: Prentice Hall.

4

Joining Up the Thinking

In this chapter we will consider:

- Why we need joined-up thinking
- How to construct the framework for joined-up thinking
- How to interpret the joined-up thinking framework
- Frequently asked questions
- An activity that you might undertake to help you improve your skill
- Recommended reading.

Why we need joined-up thinking

When planning, there is a real risk that the task is approached in such a way that although the required analysis is completed, there is a failure to see the connections between the different analyses.

Joined-up thinking is all about structuring the approach to analysis in such a way that a comparison between segments is facilitated and the choices about what to focus on within segments is also facilitated. That is, if approached in the right way, consideration can be given to how competitive one is in any one segment, as well as how competitive one is for each opportunity in a segment.

Joined-up thinking thus facilitates:

- Identification of the priority patient segments – the priority as determined by the segment's overall attractiveness. An attractive segment is likely to be one which presents a lot of opportunity and in which you are competitive for this opportunity. However, it could also be one where you are confident of your ability to create the opportunity and/or improve your position to become competitive for the opportunity.
- Identification of the priority opportunities – that is, it also helps you identify, within the segment, those opportunities which are best for the company and your product because you either have, or can acquire, the strengths to take advantage of them.
- Ultimately it helps ensure that the tactics are driven by the strategy, the forecast is driven by the strategy, and the strategy is based on the best fit between what you have or could acquire and the environment in which you are competing.

How to construct the framework for joined-up thinking

To integrate and cross-analyse all the information you have collected in your external analysis and internal analysis, a number of different marketing concepts can be applied (see Figure 4.1).

I recommend using two traditional marketing techniques – the strategic decision grid and the SWOT analysis (also frequently referred to as a TOWS analysis or OTSW analysis).

- The strategic decision grid maps each segment in terms of the opportunity that exists in a segment against the company's ability to take advantage of that opportunity (i.e. the competitive position). It also communicates the relative value of each segment – see Figure 4.2.
- SWOT analysis is a technique that combines all the information from the different audits to help you consider what you have learnt about each segment and use this understanding as a basis for decision-making – see figure 4.3.

CONSTRUCT A STRATEGIC DECISION GRID

1   The first thing to do is to create separate lists of the opportunities and threats that have been identified for each market segment. *Put the opportunities and threats list in order of importance* so that the most important factor is at the top, and the least important factor at the bottom. You should have in total about ten or twelve factors per segment. If it is longer than this, it will be difficult to work with and probably reflects a lack of hard thinking about the market in which you wish to be in, or are operating in. Note these factors were derived from the market analysis and environmental analysis.

2   Then move on to the strengths and weaknesses. These come from *within*; that is, from the product itself or from the company. Construct a list for each segment in exactly the same way as you did for the opportunities and threats. Once again, list them in order of their importance. Your list of strengths and weaknesses will be drawn from the brand audit.

Concepts	Phase 1	Phase 2	Phase 3	Phase 4
Product life cycle	Introduction	Growth	Maturity	Decline
Ansoff growth matrix	Product development	Market development	Market penetration	Diversification and alliances
Boston Consulting Group portfolio matrix	Problem child	Stars	Cash cows	Dogs

FIGURE 4.1   MARKETING CONCEPTS

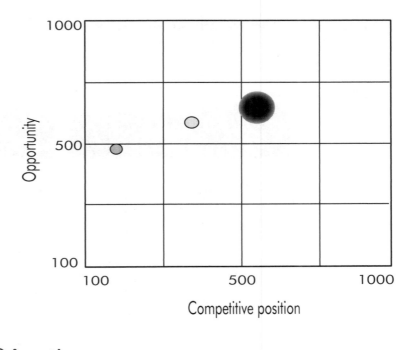

FIGURE 4.2   EXAMPLE STRATEGIC DECISION GRID

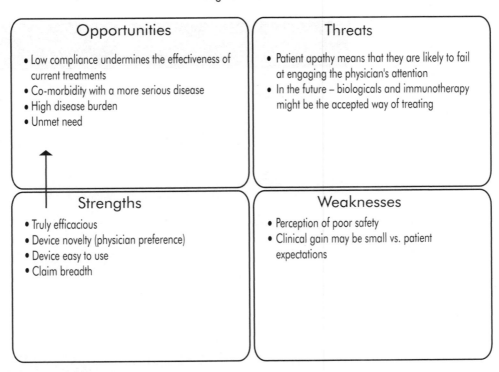

FIGURE 4.3   EXAMPLE SWOT ANALYSIS

3. You now have two lists of factors (a list of opportunities and threats, and a list of strengths and weaknesses) for each segment. All the factors listed are not of equal importance or significance. Some will be more important/significant than others.

TABLE 4.1   FRAMEWORK FOR ANALYSIS (SEGMENT 3)

Opportunity and threats factors (in rank order of importance)	Weight
1. Unmet need	25
2. High disease burden	25
3. Co-morbidity with more serious disease	17
4. Low compliance undermines the effectiveness of current treatments	17
5. Patient apathy means that they are likely to fail at engaging the physician's attention	12
6. In the future biologicals and immunotherapy might be the accepted way of treating	4
Total	100

Strengths and weaknesses factors (in rank order of importance)	Weight
1. Truly efficacious	25
2. Device novelty (physician preference)	20
3. Device easy to use	15
4. Claim breadth	15
5. Clinical gain may be small vs. patient expectations	10
6. Perception of poor safety	15
Total	100

4. *Choose one of the segments* and decide how much more important one factor is than another. *Allocate 100 points across the factors to represent their relative importance.* Table 4.1 is an example of how this can be done. You have now weighted the list and can move from your list of opportunities and threats to your list of strengths and weaknesses. Repeat this weightings exercise for the opportunities and threats and strengths and weaknesses in each segment.

5. Now move on to scoring the factors. A scoring scale appears below – see Table 4.2.

6. If you multiply the score by the weight, you will end up with a weighted score for the opportunities and threats factors in each segment, and for the strengths and weaknesses factors in each segment. The sum of the scores across all the opportunities and threats gives you the overall opportunity score for each segment. Similarly the sum of the scores across all the strengths and weaknesses factors gives you an overall competitiveness score for each segment. See Table 4.3 for an illustration.

7. To see graphically where each of your segments falls on the strategic decision grid, map the total score across all opportunities and threats against the total score for all strengths and weaknesses, for each segment. The size of the segment circle should reflect the relative value of each segment, as predicted at the end of the planning period – refer back to Figure 4.1 for an illustration.

TABLE 4.2   SCORING SCALES

SCORE	Opportunities and threats
10	Factor represents a significant opportunity
7	Factor represents an opportunity
4	Factor represents a threat
1	Factor represents a significant threat

SCORE	Strengths and weaknesses
10	Factor represents a significant strength
7	Factor represent a strength
4	Factor represents a weakness
1	Factor represents a significant weakness

TABLE 4.3   SEGMENT SCORES (SEGMENT 3)

Opportunity and threats factors (in rank order of importance)	Weight	Score	Weighted Score
1. Unmet need	25	10	250
2. High disease burden	25	1	25
3. Co-morbidity with more serious disease	17	10	170
4. Low compliance undermines the effectiveness of current treatments	17	7	119
5. Patient apathy means that they are likely to fail at engaging the physician's attention	12	7	84
6. In the future – biologicals and immunotherapy might be the accepted way of treating	4	4	16
Total	100	39	664

Strengths and weaknesses factors (in rank order of importance)	Weight	Score	Weighted Score
1. Truly efficacious	25	10	250
2. Device novelty (physician preference)	20	7	140
3. Device easy to use	15	7	105
4. Claim breadth	15	7	105
5. Clinical gain may be small vs. patient expectations	10	4	40
6. Perception of poor safety	15	1	15
Total	100	36	655

How to interpret the joined-up thinking framework

1. Start with the strategic decision grid. This is a visual representation of the absolute and relative attractiveness of each segment. The scoring system that has been applied means that:
   - Any segment that falls on or above the mid-point on the y-axis is attractive in terms of the opportunity that it proffers. The score of 450 is the point at which the segment represents an average opportunity.
   - Any segment that falls on or above 450 on the x-axis demonstrates that you are either as competitive as or more competitive than the other players in your market. This is because a score of 450 on the x-axis represents the point at which you are as competitive as the majority of other players in this market.
   - Any segment that exhibits a below average on the y-axis is signalling the fact that the barriers to accessing the opportunity that exists are significant. The higher the negative score, the more significant the barriers.
   - Any segment that exhibits a below average on the x-axis is signalling the fact that you're currently at a competitive disadvantage when compared to the other players in this market.
   - The size of the circle illustrates the relative segment value. The bigger the circle, the higher the value of the segment.
2. Now move on to the SWOT analysis. First and foremost you should describe the opportunities and threats before you describe the strengths and weaknesses. This is because when presenting the SWOT analysis, it makes sense to communicate the environment that one is competing in, in advance of talking about whether, or not, one is competitive in that environment, and for what reasons.
3. Review your SWOT analysis. Initially you are interested in initially deciding which opportunity(ies) you are interested in taking advantage of. This opportunity then provides the context for the rest of your review.
4. In order to 'choose' the opportunity(ies) you are going to have to consider whether or not you are competitive for that opportunity, or could become competitive for the opportunity. Ask yourself:
   (a) Which success factors and product attributes are implicated by the opportunity?
   (b) Are they currently strengths or weaknesses?
   (c) If they are weaknesses, are these weaknesses that I can realistically overcome? It is obviously going to be easier to play to one's strengths than correct a weakness – so there is a need to think through what might or might not be possible very carefully.
5. As soon as you are satisfied that you have identified one or more opportunities that you have a realistic chance of competing for, you need to start reviewing the threats.
   (a) Identify which threats are likely to have the greatest impact on the selected opportunity(ies).
   (b) Are these threats that you can do anything about? For example, if the threat is the size of the customer base (i.e. it is very large), then you cannot minimize or eliminate that threat. However, if the threat is an attitude or a belief, then one could argue that this is something that can be changed with time given sufficient resources.
6. As you think through what might and might not be possible you are building your understanding of the choices that you have, i.e. which opportunities you could focus on.
   (a) Which success factors and product attributes would need to be leveraged to succeed with these opportunities?

(b) Which threats could you try to manage to maximize the size of the opportunity?

7. Identify the key factors required for long-term success in each patient segment. For each of these prioritized opportunities and threats, brainstorm what are the success factors that will be required to take advantage of the opportunity or manage the threat to ensure successful commercialization of the product (see Figure 4.4).

8. Once you have a comprehensive list of 'success factors', review the list and select only the most important (typically somewhere between six and eight). You have now completed the first step in determining the factors that will be critical for success.

EXAMPLE

CHOLESTEROL-LOWERING AGENTS FACED A MARKET THAT HAD THE FOLLOWING CHARACTERISTICS: PHYSICIANS AND PATIENTS KNEW LITTLE ABOUT THE IMPORTANCE OF CHOLESTEROL AND THE IMPLICATIONS OF HAVING TOO 'HIGH' CHOLESTEROL AND/OR HOW TO RECOGNIZE IT; THERE WERE NO ACCEPTED TREATMENT GUIDELINES; PATIENTS WEREN'T IN THE PHYSICIAN'S OFFICE; REGULATORY AGENCIES WEREN'T CONVINCED ABOUT TREATMENT BENEFITS. MERCK WITH MEVACOR UNDERSTOOD WHAT WAS REQUIRED TO SUCCEED. THIS INCLUDED THE ABILITY TO: 'DEFINE THE DISEASE', INTRODUCE A DIAGNOSTIC, GET THE THOUGHT LEADERS ON BOARD, CREATE PATIENT AWARENESS THAT THEY MIGHT HAVE A PROBLEM, AND SO ON.

9. Now you should reflect on your company's ability to address these success factors. Avoid being tempted to describe what you wish to be true – try to be as honest as possible. Finally, decide which of these is critical to success – no more than five!

10. This review process is important and precedes the strategic objective setting and strategy formulation process. Setting strategic objectives and formulating the strategy is covered in the next chapter.

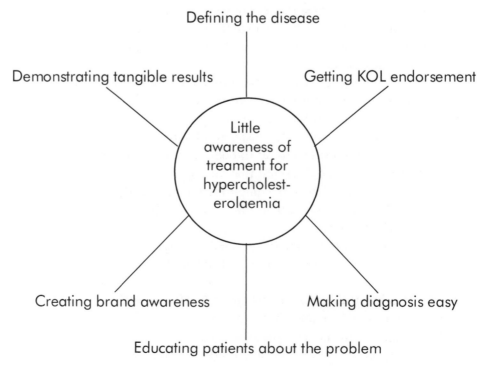

FIGURE 4.4   EXAMPLE 'SUCCESS FACTOR' BRAINSTORM

Frequently asked questions

1. **Why should I need to choose between one opportunity and another? Why could I not take advantage of them both?** If you have the necessary capabilities and resources to compete for two different opportunities, then you may well decide to do so. However, in many situations it is better to do one thing well than too many things badly. Here are my thoughts as to why you would consider one opportunity in preference to another:
    (a) because you are more competitive for that opportunity than you are for the other opportunity
    (b) because the opportunity is 'worth more' than the alternative opportunity
    (c) because you believe that through market development or market expansion you have the possibility of maximizing the size of that opportunity whereas the alternative opportunity is as big as it is going to be.

2. **If a threat is something that limits or constrains one's ability to access the market potential then why shouldn't I have a strategy to manage each threat?** Irrespective of the size of company you are working for and the amount of resources that you have, you need to make sure that you are using your resources wisely. This in turn means that there is little point in addressing or managing threats unless you are well placed to take advantage of the related opportunity. There are many examples of companies within the industry investing in market development and/or expansion only to see the competition walk off with the sales benefit.

    Here are some questions you might ask yourself to help you prioritize which threats to focus on:
    (a) Is the threat affecting the opportunity that I want to focus on?
    (b) Is the threat something I believe I am well placed to manage (i.e. have I the required capabilities)?
    (c) How confident am I that you can affect the threat?
    (d) Can I survive if I don't take steps to protect myself from the threat?

3. **How does the weighting that I apply to the factors affect the segment's overall attractiveness?** Factors with a high weight skew the results either positively or negatively. Thus it is my recommendation that you use your weighting as follows:
    (a) When weighting opportunities and threats, apply a high weight to those factors that you have less influence over, i.e. that you cannot change. Thus, if the factor exists, and its existence is favourable, then this will positively affect the segment's total 'opportunity score' and vice versa. Do not allow the nature of the factor (i.e. whether it is an opportunity or threat) to influence the weighting.
    (b) When weighting strengths and weaknesses, apply a high weight to those factors that are greater determinants of success than the other factors. Do not allow the nature of the factor (i.e. whether it is a strength or weakness) to influence the weighting.

An activity that you might undertake to help you improve your skill

Take an example of a SWOT analysis from any plan that exists within your organization. Can you work out how the capabilities and/or product attributes help or hinder you competitively? How would you explain this?

If you were the product manager of this plan, which of the opportunities would you focus on? And why? What in your view are the significant issues? And why? Can you prioritize the issues? On what basis have you done this?

Recommended reading

Lidstone, J. and MacLennan, J. (1999) *Marketing Planning for the Pharmaceutical Industry*, Hampshire: Gower.

Schulz, E. (2000) *The Marketing Game: How the World's Best Companies Play to Win*, London: Kogan Page Ltd.

5

Formulating the Strategy

In this chapter we will consider:

- What is meant by strategy?
- What are the key ingredients in formulating the strategy?
- How to approach the development of strategic options
- Frequently asked questions
- An activity to help you test your skills
- Definitions of terms used
- Recommended reading.

What is meant by strategy?

Good planning demands that you know where you are headed for and those logical alternatives for getting there are explored. These alternatives are referred to as strategies.

Thus, when we refer to strategy, we are talking about a game plan. It is a broad statement describing how we intend to achieve the strategic objectives set out in the marketing plan. Your strategic objectives can be achieved in a number of ways.

For example, the strategic objective *to increase volume of sales by 10%* can be achieved by:

1. increasing sales in a particular segment (either by growing the segment or taking share from the competition) or
2. penetrating a completely new segment (either by promoting the product on its existing attributes or by repositioning the product for that segment).

These are different strategies.

A strategy defines the route selected from a number of choices that are available. A strategy enables you to:

- integrate all the elements of the business that are required for the product to be marketed successfully
- direct the allocation of resources and effort required
- be selective as to the means of achieving the goals.

What are the key ingredients in formulating the strategy?

THE STRATEGIC OBJECTIVES

You need to know where you are heading before you can explore alternative ways of getting there.

THE STRATEGIC OPTIONS

These are the alternative routes (or approaches) that you might take to achieve your strategic objectives. Each strategic option may involve different target customers.

FORECASTING REVENUE AND INVESTMENT

Each strategy will require investment. Typically the nature of the investment varies according to the strategy, as do the results (i.e. anticipated future size of the market, your patient share and the associated revenue).

TARGETING

In Chapter 1 we focused on market segmentation, namely, the identification of distinct need-states with similar characteristics and needs that can be selectively and separately targeted. The purpose of identifying the need-state and the associated patient segments and selecting one of them to target is twofold. First, any pharmaceutical company, however large, cannot effectively target all identifiable market segments (i.e. physician treatment goals) with one product. Some treatment goals will be better served by the competitors. Second, it would be a huge waste of your resources to pursue segments with low profitability. Instead, your focus should be on the segments where you have or can attain sustainable competitive advantage, and the desired sales revenue and market share growth. Strategy formulation is about making choices: choices regarding which need-state, which patient segments, and choices regarding which issues and opportunities to focus on in the target segments. Note that targeting is not the same thing as 'niching' the product. It is important to understand that by defining a 'target need-state' you are not excluding others; it merely describes the 'core' need that your brand is going to satisfy.

How to approach the development of strategic options

1. Develop ideas on how you might express a clearly definable target. The ideas should be both quantitative (e.g. a billion dollar brand) and qualitative (change the treatment paradigm). Quantitative targets have the advantage of being precise and specific whereas qualitative strategic objectives are often more compelling because they create vivid images of what success will look like.
2. Decide on the strategic objectives. Without strategic objectives, you have no chance of creating your future; you can only react to it. The strategic objectives should be both qualitative and quantitative expressions of the target. They are there to generate the commitment needed to achieve high performance. The qualitative component needs to bring the quantitative numbers to life. For the qualitative component you can adopt one or more approaches:

- Create a goal focused on defeating a competitor. This approach taps into the basic human motivation that people don't like to survive, they like to win (e.g. beat Brand X).
- Define an image that means the same thing to everyone (e.g. to be the IBM of the pharmaceutical industry).
- Define the endpoint as the internal transformation that is required (e.g. Simply Better in every way).

3 Ask yourself:
- Are they stretching, and challenging?
- Do they have a finish line and a specific timeframe for their achievement?
- Are they achievable? The concept of the strategic objectives being 'achievable' is important, which is why they are typically only formulated once you have a good understanding of the market and your competitive situation.
- Do they express what success will look like? Take the example of Alpharma's strategic objective: 'To take credit for making medicines affordable, available and understandable'.

4 Now you need to describe how you might go about achieving these objectives. Could one of the variables be which segment you should target? Could another variable be the approach you take within the target segment? That is, market expansion, market development and/or market penetration? Do you have more than one product or offering for different segments? If yes, then this could be another variable. Whether you are using price or differentiation as the basis for competing in the target segment is also something worth thinking about and describing in your strategy.

5 To help you with the decision as to what your strategic options might be, you should consider the following:

   a **Future market size and potential of each segment:** What is the actual and potential size of each segment? In terms of patient numbers? In terms of value? Are you forecasting that the 'served' market will grow or decline over the next few years? Consider your answers to these questions for each market segment. Now rank the segments according to superiority, equivalence and inferiority (see table 5.1).

   b **The characteristics of each segment?** Is there unmet need or dissatisfaction with existing products? What are the attitudes and beliefs of the decision-makers and key influencers? Would you be able to take advantage of them, or do you need to shape them? What are the barriers to success? How easy will these be to overcome? In other words, what are the issues? Consider your answers to these questions for each market

TABLE 5.1   FUTURE MARKET SIZE AND POTENTIAL

	Segment 1	Segment 2	Segment 3, etc.
Patient numbers (actual)			
Patient numbers (potential)			
Segment value (actual)			
Segment value (potential)			
Market forecast (+/-)			

TABLE 5.2   SEGMENT CHARACTERISTICS

	Segment 1	Segment 2	Segment 3, etc.
Level of unmet need/dissatisfaction			
Attitudes and beliefs of decision-makers			
Attitudes and beliefs of influencers			
Ease with which barriers can be overcome			

segment and again rank the segments according to superiority, equivalence and inferiority (see Table 5.2).

(c) **Questions regarding your product and how competitive it is:** Does the product you have meet the needs of the patient segment? Do you have a point of difference? Where are you exposed? Consider your answers to these questions for each patient segment and rank the segments according to superiority, equivalence and inferiority (see Table 5.3).

(d) **Do you have the necessary capabilities?** What outside of the product profile will generate sustainable competitive advantage to help you compete for share in each patient segment? Where is your exposure? Consider your answers to these questions for each patient segment. Now rank the segments according to superiority, equivalence and inferiority (see Table 5.4).

(e) **Questions about the level of investment associated with competing in each segment:** How much will you need to invest to compete effectively in each segment? What is the likely return? What level of risk is there associated with investment in each patient segment? Consider your answers to these questions for each patient segment. Now rank the segments according to superiority, equivalence and inferiority (Table 5.5).

6. Summarize your findings – see Table 5.6. Then draw your conclusions as to what your strategic options might be (see Table 5.6).

TABLE 5.3   HOW COMPETITIVE IS YOUR PRODUCT?

	Segment 1	Segment 2	Segment 3, etc.
Extent to which product satisfies the 'need'			
Extent to which product delivers an advantage over the competition			
Is the competitive advantage sustainable?			
Do any of the product features enable you to leverage the unmet emotional needs?			

TABLE 5.4 DO WE HAVE THE NECESSARY CAPABILITIES?

	Segment 1	Segment 2	Segment 3, etc.
Do we have the necessary capabilities?			
Number of capabilities that give you competitive advantage			
Degree of confidence that this advantage is sustainable			

TABLE 5.5 WHAT IS THE REQUIRED LEVEL OF INVESTMENT?

	Segment 1	Segment 2	Segment 3, etc.
Level of investment required			
Confidence in likely return of that investment (i.e. level of risk)			
Extent to which investment required is up front			

TABLE 5.6 SEGMENT OVERALL ATTRACTIVENESS

	Segment 1	Segment 2	Segment 3, etc.
Future market size and potential			
How competitive is your			
Do we have the necessary capabilities?			
What is the required level of investment?			
Segment overall attractiveness			

7. For each strategic option work out the investment required, and over what time, to the required level of detail. Examples of the types of investment categories that are typically required appear in Table 5.7.

TABLE 5.7   EXAMPLE INVESTMENT FORECAST

	Yr – 3	Yr – 2	Yr – 1	Current	Yr + 1	Yr + 2	Yr + 3	Yr + 4	Yr + 5
Agency Fee									
Conferences/meeting									
Mailing									
PR and Med. Ed.									
Patient Support									
Product Support									
Medical Sponsorship									
Samples									
Market Research									
Total Promotion									
Phase 4 Costs									
Other Marketing									
Total Marketing									
Medical									
Regulatory									
Total R and D									
Selling									
Administration									

8. Now start working on your forecast. Make sure that your forecast is determined in the light of the assumptions that you are making about the level of the investment, the timing of that investment, the issues and/or opportunities that you are going to be focusing on and your starting position. Ensure that all assumptions you are making in connection with the forecast are explicit.

TIPS ON HOW TO APPROACH THE FORECAST

ALWAYS START WITH THE MARKET

1. IDEALLY START WITH THE SIZE OF THE TREATED PATIENT POPULATION IN EACH TARGET SEGMENT.
2. OVERLAY YOUR CONCLUSIONS FROM YOUR ENVIRONMENTAL ANALYSIS (REFER TO CHAPTER 2). IS YOUR TARGET PATIENT SEGMENT LIKELY TO GROW FASTER OR SLOWER IN THE FUTURE COMPARED TO ITS HISTORIC BEHAVIOUR AND, IF SO, WHY? IS THE AVERAGE DRUG TREATMENT VALUE PER PATIENT LIKELY TO CHANGE? IF SO, WHY?
3. NOW CONSIDER THE PROPOSED STRATEGY. DOES THIS STRATEGY INVOLVE CHANGING THE SIZE OF THE TREATED POPULATION IN THE TARGET PATIENT SEGMENT? IF YES, ADJUST YOUR MARKET FORECAST ACCORDINGLY.
4. NOW CONSIDER THE FUTURE SEGMENT VALUE. IS THERE ANYTHING THAT YOU ARE DOING THAT WILL IMPACT THE AVERAGE TREATMENT VALUE OF A PATIENT? IF SO, MAKE THE NECESSARY ADJUSTMENTS.

NOW MOVE ON TO YOUR LIKELY SHARE OF THAT MARKET

WHEN YOU START FORECASTING YOUR FUTURE MARKET SHARE, I STRONGLY RECOMMEND THAT YOU APPROACH THIS TASK BY CONSIDERING WHAT THE RESULT MIGHT BE IN A NUMBER OF DIFFERENT WAYS. IRRESPECTIVE OF THE APPROACH YOU TAKE, ALWAYS REFER BACK TO YOUR EARLIER ANALYSIS (REFER TO CHAPTERS 2 AND 3); THE MARKET CHARACTERISTICS OF YOUR TARGET PATIENT SEGMENT AND YOUR COMPETITIVE POSITION SHOULD INFORM THE FORECAST.

1. ONE APPROACH IS TO REFER TO ANALOGOUS MARKET SITUATIONS. THESE DO NOT HAVE TO BE WITHIN THE SAME THERAPEUTIC AREA. RATHER, WHAT IS IMPORTANT IS THAT THE MARKET CHARACTERISTICS AND THE COMPETITOR SITUATIONS ARE SIMILAR. HOW DID THE NEW ENTRANT PERFORM? HOW QUICKLY DID THEY GAIN MARKET SHARE? BASED ON SEVERAL SUCH EXAMPLES, HOW WELL MIGHT YOUR PRODUCT DO? AND HOW QUICKLY? MAKE SURE YOU ARE ABLE TO EXPLAIN/SUPPORT YOUR ASSUMPTIONS.
2. A DIFFERENT APPROACH IS TO START WITH THE NUMBER OF POTENTIAL PRESCRIBERS IN YOUR MARKET. USE A SPREADSHEET TO THEN DEVELOP A FORECAST MODEL BY ANSWERING THE FOLLOWING QUESTIONS:
   A HOW MANY OF THESE PRESCRIBERS ARE YOU PLANNING TO REACH?
   B OF THOSE THAT YOU REACH, HOW MANY WILL BE SUFFICIENTLY INTERESTED IN YOUR TREATMENT CONCEPT (PRODUCT) TO ACTUALLY TRY IT?
   C HOW MANY OF THOSE THAT TRY IT ARE LIKELY TO CONTINUE PRESCRIBING IT?
   D HOW MANY OF THOSE THAT START PRESCRIBING IT ARE LIKELY TO PRESCRIBE IT MORE OFTEN THAN ANY OF THE OTHER COMPETITOR PRODUCTS?
   E THEN ESTIMATE THE NUMBER OF PRESCRIPTIONS THAT A 'USER' IS LIKELY TO GENERATE WITHIN AN APPROPRIATE TIME PERIOD (E.G. A WEEK/A MONTH ETC.) AND THE NUMBER OF PRESCRIPTIONS THAT A 'LOYALIST' IS LIKELY TO GENERATE WITHIN THIS SAME TIME PERIOD.
   F HOW IS THIS PATTERN LIKELY TO CHANGE OVER TIME?
   G WHAT IS THE ANSWER? CONVERT THIS INTO PATIENT SHARE OVER TIME
3. SOPHISTICATED EPIDEMIOLOGY-BASED MODELS ARE ANOTHER WAY TO GO. THESE REQUIRE GOOD PREVALENCE AND INCIDENCE DATA AND AN UNDERSTANDING OF HOW MANY PEOPLE WITH THE CONDITION EVENTUALLY GET INTO THE HEALTHCARE SYSTEM, GET DRUG TREATMENT AND ARE TREATED WITH THE APPROPRIATE TYPE OF MEDICATION. THEY TYPICALLY USE THE CONCEPT OF PREFERENCE SHARES (WHICH ARE BASED ON THE PRODUCT PROFILE ONLY) TO ARRIVE AT A PATIENT SHARE FORECAST.

9. Finally, examine which option offers the greatest potential revenues. In the near term? And over time? Which option is the most profitable? In the near term? And over time? Which option is associated with the least risk? These are the sorts of question that you might ask yourself before deciding on a preferred route.
10. Once you have decided the preferred route, check your recommendation using the following checklist of questions:

- Have I articulated a clear strategy for achieving the strategic objectives?
- Is the strategy convincing?
- Is the strategy appropriate to the stage of the product life cycle, competitor's strategies and the state of the economy?
- Do I have clear criteria for choosing my target segment?
- Is there sufficient investment planned to achieve the strategic objectives?

Frequently asked questions

- **I'm convinced about what we need to do – why do I need to go through the effort of describing and evaluating different options?** You need to be able to persuade other people in the organization that you have considered alternate routes to achieving the strategic objectives and that the one that you are recommending is the most suitable based on good business arguments.
- **The word 'strategy' is used in many different contexts – can you provide any guidelines for how it should be used?** There are many different types and levels of strategy, including corporate strategy, operational strategy, marketing strategy, product strategy, distribution strategy, marketing communications strategy, advertising strategy etc.

    Probably the easiest way to think about strategy is as a cascade. One person's strategy becomes another person's objectives as you go down the line of managers. Any strategy should always be in response to an objective.
- **What is the difference between strategy and objectives?** An objective is an end state, an outcome. A strategy is a means of achieving this outcome.
- **What are the key components of any strategic option?** The components of any marketing strategy should make reference to the product(s), the patient segment(s) and customers, the strengths that will be used for advantage, the resources, the scope/scale of investment and the timing.

An activity to help you test your skills

Without referring to the text earlier in this chapter, try to answer the following questions:

- What would you look for in a marketing strategy?
- What are the key components?
- What would make it incomplete?

Now turn to any recent strategic brand plan which you know failed to deliver against its strategic objectives. What were the strategic objectives? What strategic options were explored? Why were they rejected? What questions might have been asked to expose the vulnerabilities of the recommended strategy?

Definitions of terms used

- **Strategic objectives:**
  - — describe success
  - — serve as a basis for the strategy, the product position and the marketing objectives
  - — should be succinct and clear
  - — should be motivating for everyone involved in the marketing and support of the product, a positive picture of long-term success
  - — a 'stretch goal' for the organization.
- **Strategy:** A description of how you will achieve your strategic objectives. It typically makes reference to which segments, which products and through which mechanism, e.g. market expansion vs. market penetration.
- **Strategic options:** Describe the choices that are available to you. Each option describes one possible route to achieving the strategic objectives.
- **Target customers:** Clinical or non-clinical people who it is believed will have a significant influence on prescribing, either directly or indirectly, and are key to implementing your strategy.

Recommended reading

Corstjens, Marcel (1991) *Marketing Strategy in the Pharmaceutical Industry*, London: Chapman & Hall.

Garvin, David A. and Roberto, Michael A. (2001) 'What you don't know about making decisions', *Harvard Business Review*, September: 108–116.

6

Developing the Brand Strategy

In this chapter we will consider:

- What is meant by brand strategy?
- What are the key ingredients in formulating the brand strategy?
- Guidelines for writing a product/brand position statement
- How to develop the brand strategy
- Guidelines for implementing brand strategy
- Guidelines for market research
- Frequently asked questions
- An activity to help you test your skills
- Definitions of terms used
- Recommended reading.

What is meant by brand strategy?

In its entirety the brand strategy defines the associations that will be important to build in the customer's mind (functional, emotional, conscious and unconscious). These associations are based on the insight that you have into the conceptual target's attitudes and beliefs. These associations are intended to describe what the brand stands for.

The brand strategy provides the direction for the distinctive delivery of the brand promise. All aspects of brand delivery, including the communication efforts, should support the brand strategy. In pharmaceutical marketing there are three key components to the brand strategy – the brand essence and how this is translated into the more descriptive brand values, and brand position.

WHAT IS MEANT BY BRAND ESSENCE?

The brand essence defines in one statement what it is that the brand stands for. It summarizes the key meaning we want associated with the brand. It is the result of integrating all the key product attributes, as well as the intangible aspects of the brand. It talks to the critical insight and can only be derived once you understand which associations need to be built in the customer's mind (functional, emotional, conscious and unconscious).

WHAT IS MEANT BY BRAND VALUES?

The primary attributes that customers and consumers identify with the brand and the predominant personality characteristics that reflect the way customers and consumers perceive the brand. They provide tonal and emotional continuity, directly and indirectly, to the brand delivery.

WHAT IS MEANT BY BRAND POSITION?

Brand position vs. positioning – what is the difference? Does it matter? Often these terms are used interchangeably, the implication being that they fundamentally mean the same thing. In order to leverage the full value from these strategic marketing concepts, however, it is necessary to distinguish between them.

Initially Aaker defined positioning as 'the art and science of fitting the product or service to one or more segments of the broad market, in such a way as to set it meaningfully apart from the competition'. Reis and Trout, however, adopted another approach. While they acknowledge that 'positioning starts with a product', they conclude that 'positioning is not what you do to the product. Positioning is what you do to the mind of the prospect.' I tend to agree.

The brand position statement articulates the strategic intentions for the product, while positioning describes what has been achieved, and also refers to the activities driving it. Too many companies approach their strategies as if the competition does not exist. Customers have a repertoire from which they make their choice. If a product holds a clear and undisputed slot within the repertoire, the customer's mind has no room to accommodate another in the same or similar position and thus will either discount it or reject it outright.

For the purposes of planning, therefore, let us agree that positioning indicates the brand's image in the market place (that is, both the positive and negative associations perceived to be related to a product), and that the brand position is the position that you want it to have in the market place – typically this includes a description of the people, situations or circumstances in which the product should be prescribed, its benefit, and the reasons to believe the benefit. The difference is subtle, but it is important that you are able to make the distinction, because of the implications.

The implications of this distinction shifts the emphasis from articulating the brand position statement correctly in the brand plan towards ensuring that all your communications and actions are completely aligned with the strategic brand position. Clear and consistent compelling messages are the only means to achieve the desired brand position. This is irrespective of who or what delivers the communication – be it an advert, a company representative, the packaging, a key opinion leader, the CEO or indeed the receptionist – it all contributes to the customer's perception of the brand's positioning.

What are the key ingredients in formulating the brand strategy?

The key ingredients of any brand strategy are the definition and articulation of the following: the target need-state; the conceptual target; the critical customer insight; the core brand values; the brand essence; the product position statement; the key messages. Each of these components is now described further.

TARGET NEED-STATE

The need-state is usually described as the physician treatment goal that your brand is targeting. The need-state typically arises as a result of the patient–physician interaction.

THE CONCEPTUAL TARGET

The conceptual target is usually described in demographic terms or in psychographic terms and refers to the group of physicians (or customers) that has the greatest potential to prescribe your product. Occasionally the conceptual target includes both the physician and the patient. Of course, you are hoping that all physicians will prescribe your product – but this does not mean that you should include 'all physicians' in your description of the conceptual target. The conceptual target does not exclude other physicians (and/or situations); it merely describes the core group. You need to be specific and knowledgeable about this core group to develop effective communication.

THE CRITICAL INSIGHT

The most deeply held desire, want, hope or fear of the conceptual target that the brand can best fulfil.

THE CORE BRAND VALUES

Vital elements of the brand that are intrinsic to its existence and cannot be compromised. They provide tonal and emotional continuity, directly and indirectly, to all communications.

THE BRAND ESSENCE

We have to crystallize in a single idea, capture the very essence of what we wish the brand to stand for and, in doing so, we must strike the right balance between standout and significance. To pinpoint that vital idea, we need to look deep into customers' minds (the conceptual target) and grasp the true value of the brand from their perspective.

THE BRAND POSITION STATEMENT

A brand position statement describes:

1. the rational associations that we believe will communicate why the product is appropriate for the target patient population
2. in emotional terms, the relevance of these rational associations.

A strategic brand position statement is not 'Brand X will be prescribed first line in indication Y'. The strategic positioning of any brand requires you to specify the following (see Figure 6.1 and the description of the process).

THE KEY MESSAGES

These are the compelling arguments that convince the physician (or the target customers) to prescribe the product so the product is prescribed as intended and for the reasons that were intended.

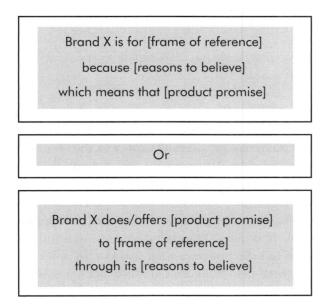

FIGURE 6.1   FUTURE MARKET SIZE AND POTENTIAL

Guidelines for writing a brand position statement

THE 'FRAME OF REFERENCE'

The frame of reference is particularly important for new products because it gives physicians, other healthcare professionals and patients a context for the new medication. The frame of reference can be a need (e.g. Tylenol is a painkiller), it can be a description of the target market profile (e.g. Fosamax is for post-menopausal women), it can be a product class (e.g. Cozaar is an ACE inhibitor) etc. The different approaches are covered in some detail below. The frame of reference is typically a point of 'parity' association. The frame of reference is important because no product can be marketed to a population 'en masse'.

Among the different approaches you can take to describing your frame of reference are:

- **By use or application:** This is a very effective approach when the competition is outside the product category or the product is an innovation, that is, it is creating a new category.

EXAMPLES

WHEN BLACK & DECKER INTRODUCED THEIR SNAKELIGHT® AS AN INNOVATIVE SOLUTION TO THE PROBLEM OF TRYING TO HOLD A FLASHLIGHT WHILE WORKING, THE COMMUNICATION SHOWED THE PRODUCT BEING USED IN VARIOUS NON-OBVIOUS WAYS.

WHEN 3M POST-IT NOTES® WERE LAUNCHED ALMOST TWO DECADES AGO, THERE WAS NO PERCEIVED FRAME OF REFERENCE FOR USAGE, NEED OR BENEFIT. THE COMPANY HAD TO FIRST ESTABLISH A RANGE OF USES AND APPLICATIONS THROUGH DEMONSTRATION, SAMPLING AND TRIAL IN ORDER TO CREATE A VALUE FOR THE PRODUCT.

CAMPBELL'S SOUP POSITIONED ITSELF AS A LUNCHTIME PRODUCT AND UTILIZED NOONTIME RADIO EXTENSIVELY TO REINFORCE THIS.

KELLOGG'S NUTRI-GRAIN BARS ARE POSITIONED AGAINST BREAKFAST, WHEN YOU'RE IN A RUSH AND NEED FUEL-ON-THE-HOOF.

THE BELL TELEPHONE COMPANY HAS ASSOCIATED LONG-DISTANCE CALLING WITH COMMUNICATING WITH LOVED ONES AS EVIDENCED BY ITS 'REACH OUT AND TOUCH SOMEONE' CAMPAIGNS.

- **By product class:** There are two options within this category. The first and most unconventional approach is to use the frame of reference to position the product against an existing or dominant class, which serves as the mental benchmark against which prospects make their decisions. Alternatively, new innovations or technologies set out to create a class in their own right, which may either live in tandem with the original class – as in butter alongside margarine – or completely usurp the original class – for example, CDs vs. vinyl records. The second alternative within this class approach is where the product itself creates a whole new class. Thus if a company has a truly new product, innovation or category, it is best to tell the prospect what it is not, in order to create new 'mind-space'. Some examples of these new categories are 'lite' beer, 'lead-free' gasoline, '2% milk' or 'sugar-free' food and drinks.

EXAMPLES

AN EXAMPLE OF THE UNCONVENTIONAL, BUT IN THIS CASE EXTREMELY SUCCESSFUL, APPROACH IS 7-UP IN THE CARBONATED SOFT DRINKS CATEGORY. ALMOST TWO-THIRDS OF ALL SODAS PURCHASED ARE COLA DRINKS. FOR 7-UP TO FIND A UNIQUE POSITION AND RELEVANCE IN CONSUMERS' MINDS, IT HAD TO IGNORE CONVENTIONAL WISDOM AND LOOK FOR AN ANCHOR OUTSIDE THE PRODUCT ITSELF. HENCE ITS POSITIONING AS 'THE FIRST ALTERNATIVE TO COLA'.

OTHER EXAMPLES WHERE THE COMPETITION – OR FRAME OF REFERENCE – COMES FROM OUTSIDE THE CLASS ARE THE 'CHEAP AND CHEERFUL' AIRLINES, WHERE THEY POSITION THEMSELVES AGAINST NOT ONLY THE BIGGER, MORE ESTABLISHED AIRLINES, BUT ALSO WHERE TRAINS AND BUSES ARE VIABLE ALTERNATIVES. HERE THE KEY DRIVER IS MORE ABOUT COST AND LESS ABOUT CONVENIENCE OR COMFORT. CONVERSELY, HIGH-SPEED TRAINS POSITION THEMSELVES RELATIVE TO CONVENTIONAL AIRLINES AS A MORE COST- AND TIME-EFFICIENT ALTERNATIVE, THE OFFER BEING THAT THE TIME SPENT IN TRAVEL COULD BE USED MORE EFFECTIVELY AND COMFORTABLY, AT A LOWER COST – THE CLASSIC TIME–VALUE DECISION TRADE-OFF. EXAMPLES WOULD BE EUROSTAR OR AMTRAK.

- **By product user:** This is where the frame of reference is based on the product users themself. When it works, a user positioning strategy is effective because it can match positioning with a segmentation strategy.

EXAMPLES

COSMETICS COMPANIES USE THIS APPROACH A LOT; NOXELL'S COVER GIRL RANGE HAD A CLEARLY DEFINED IMAGE FOR 'THE GIRL NEXT DOOR' AND BECAME THE DEFINITIVE NAME FOR 'WHOLESOME, HEALTHY (AND USUALLY BLONDE) WOMEN'. BY CONTRAST, REVLON WENT FOR 'THE MORE SOPHISTICATED WOMAN'.

OTHER EXAMPLES WOULD INCLUDE CERTAIN BEVERAGE OR FASHION BRANDS, WHICH HAVE STRONG ASSOCIATIONS WITH KNOWN *INDIVIDUALS*. NIKE'S 'JUST DO IT' IS ASSOCIATED WITH THE BEST SPORTSMEN THE WORLD OVER, STARTING WITH THEIR SMASH HIT PRODUCT 'AIR JORDANS'. THE CHOSEN ASSOCIATION MAY BE WITH IDENTIFIABLE GROUPS E.G. DEWARS, REMY-MARTIN OR MILLER LITE BEER. THUS THE COMMUNICATIONS EMPHASIZE IDENTIFICATION OR ASSOCIATION WITH A SPECIFIC INDIVIDUAL OR GROUP, WHICH COULD BE REAL OR FICTIONAL (ASPIRATIONAL).

- **By competitor:** It is also possible to have a frame of reference that positions one's brand relative to a specific competitor. This is similar to positioning by product class. However, in this case a specific competitor is singled out from the same category.

EXAMPLES

THE BEST-KNOWN EXAMPLE OF THIS IS THE CASE OF AVIS WHICH POSITIONED ITSELF AGAINST THE CAR RENTAL LEADER HERTZ BY STATING: 'AVIS IS ONLY NO 2 IN RENT-A-CARS, SO WHY GO WITH US? WE TRY HARDER.' ESTABLISHING THE 'AGAINST' POSITIONING IS A CLASSIC COMPETITIVE MANOEUVRE. IF A COMPANY ISN'T NO 1, THEN IT NEEDS TO BE THE FIRST TO OCCUPY THE NO 2 POSITION WITH CREDIBILITY. BURGER KING AND PEPSI ARE TWO OTHER CLASSIC EXAMPLES. MANY HOUSEHOLD CATEGORIES SUCH AS WASHING SOAP, KITCHEN PAPER TOWELS ETC. ALSO FALL INTO THIS CATEGORY.

THE PRODUCT PROMISE

You then need to determine the benefit that your product delivers. It can be functional – for example, powerful, safe etc. – or it can be psychological – for example, gain freedom, realize your potential etc. This is the 'so what' or 'what's in it for them'. Depending on the therapeutic area, the benefit may be geared towards the physician (i.e. why should he/she prescribe your product?) or the patient (why should he or she take your product?). The most powerful approach is finding a benefit that resonates across all customers. It needs to be relevant and compelling.

EXAMPLES

GOOD INSIGHTFUL PHARMACEUTICAL EXAMPLES HERE INCLUDE FOSAMAX, WHICH IS ALL ABOUT THE 'PRESERVATION OF GRANDMOTHER'S PHYSICAL STRENGTH', AND SERETIDE/ADVAIR FOR PATIENTS WITH COPD: 'THE PROMISE OF DAYS WHEN LIFE FEELS GOOD ENOUGH TO FORGET WORSENING LUNG FUNCTION'.

Sometimes the promise may include more than one benefit. However, the objective is to identify the most salient attributes given the frame of reference. That is, those that are the most important to the target audience and the basis for making their decisions, as competitors will find it hard to attack this head to head.

Mann and Plummer in their study of the Aspirin Wars highlight the different product promises adopted by the major players over a 100-year period. Anacin, in order to distinguish itself from Bayer and Bufferin, positioned itself as a 'formula, which combined smaller quantities of a number of highly effective pain relievers – the benefit being faster, more effective and safer relief than a large dose of a single drug'.

EXAMPLES

AN EXAMPLE IN THE COMPUTER INDUSTRY IS APPLE. WHILE THE IBM GIANT COULD NOT BE DISLODGED HEAD-ON, APPLE II'S PRODUCT PROMISE WAS AROUND ONE KEY DISTINCTION AND BENEFIT TO THE USER – AS A 'COMPUTER USING A FRIENDLY AND UNINTIMIDATING PROCESS'. CONSEQUENTLY, EVERYTHING AT APPLE, FROM ITS LOGO DOWN TO ITS DOWN-TO-EARTH FOUNDERS, UNDERSCORES THIS UNIQUE PROMISE.

BMW USE A PRODUCT ATTRIBUTE AS THE BASIS TO BUILD THEIR BRAND PROMISE – THE 'SUPERIOR HANDLING' ATTRIBUTE IS TRANSLATED INTO THE CUSTOMER BENEFIT OF 'GREATER DRIVING SATISFACTION', WHICH ULTIMATELY TRANSLATES INTO THEIR SLOGAN OF 'BMW. SHEER DRIVING PLEASURE.'

A REASON TO BELIEVE

People are generally quite logical. If you say something that makes sense, they will believe you. If you say something that doesn't make sense, or sounds like you are stretching the truth, they will be sceptical. This is why you need a reason to believe. This is the area where you need to point out what is unique or different about your offering that allows you to claim the 'benefit'. The reason to believe is one of the more compelling arguments given to support the benefit.

EXAMPLES (HYPOTHETICAL)

- FOR PARENTS WITH YOUNG CHILDREN, AMOXIL SYRUP IS THE ANTIBIOTIC THAT YOU CAN TRUST TO PROTECT THE LIVES OF YOUR LOVED ONES. THAT'S BECAUSE THE BANANA FLAVOUR DISGUISES THE TASTE OF THE ANTIBIOTIC, ENSURING THAT EVERY CHILD WILL TAKE THEIR MEDICINE, WITHOUT FUSS.
- FOR MEN AGED 18–65, VIAGRA IS THE MEDICINE THAT CAN MAKE A DIFFERENCE TO YOUR SEXUAL HEALTH. THAT'S BECAUSE IT HAS BEEN DESIGNED WITH A SENSE OF PLAYFULNESS THAT AWAKENS THE INNER FIGHTING SPIRIT AND REMINDS US OF JUST HOW GOOD LIFE CAN BE.

How to approach the development of brand strategy

Companies **sell products**; companies **market brands**. Implementing branding requires going beyond selling the product, no matter how superior the product is. The challenge with branding is to create and convey the meaning of the product. Meaning is more than description or wordsmithing, although words are one of the ways of expressing meaning. Meaning is how the product should be understood from the customer's perspective. Meaning is the stuff of brands.

EXAMPLE

DOES IT MATTER IF WE HAVE COKE OR PEPSI? YES, IT DOES, BECAUSE THE TWO HAVE VERY DIFFERENT MEANINGS. COKE IS TRADITION; IT IS A CLASSIC REFRESHMENT. PEPSI IS THE FUTURE; IT IS THE TASTE OF YOUTH AND POSSIBILITY. WHATEVER WORDS ARE USED TO EXPRESS THE DIFFERENCE, WHAT IS BEING DESCRIBED IS NOT WHAT COKE OR PEPSI *IS* SO MUCH AS WHAT THEY *STAND FOR*.

So what paradigm should guide you when putting branding into practice? Here are my recommendations:

- **Always start with the customer – not with what has been decided is the strategy, or how the agency wants to do the ads.**
- **Get to the point where you can describe the brand meaning to a target group of customers (the conceptual target).** To the point where this meaning is neither too abstract or concrete. Where it is executable but not overly encompassing. Below I describe a step-by-step approach for doing this.

1. The first thing to do is to identify your conceptual target. The conceptual target is the 'person' to whom your brand must appeal.

2. Once you have established your conceptual target, you need to decide which critical insight your brand will leverage in order to make your product meaningful to customers, to establish an intuitive bond with the customer based on profound understanding.

Digging to find the most relevant customer insight can be the most difficult and challenging task you will face in developing the brand strategy. The place to develop this profound understanding and look for potential sources of meaning is in the customer and consumer's life. By life I mean some part of the customer or consumer's everyday experience, what it is like to have, and to treat, the condition. You are looking for narrative threads that tell the story.

When we investigate the customers and consumers there are three possibilities:
- we will learn about where things are already turning out well
- we will uncover areas where things remain unresolved, and
- we will uncover areas that are turning out poorly.

The last two offer potential branding opportunities because there is always the possibility that things could turn out better. Anything that affects the customer's life or the consumer's life is by definition meaningful and relevant. And things that make for a better ending are potentially valuable. Thus any insight in which you see the possibility for meaningful, relevant value is a potential branding opportunity – provided that we can attach the product to this meaningful, relevant value. This insight is what I refer to as the critical insight.

The description of the conceptual target together with this critical insight and the target need-state is the basis for the development of the brand strategy.

3. You should seek to identify associations that cover the following areas (see Figure 6.2):

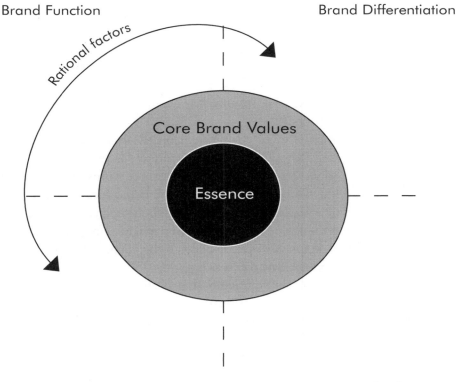

FIGURE 6.2   EXAMPLE BRAND STRATEGY

- The association that explains the role the brand will play for the conceptual target. To determine this, ask yourself: what is this brand's relevance to the conceptual target? What does it do for them? What is its benefit? This can be described in a functional way or symbolically.
- Associations that differentiate the brand from its competitors. To do this, ask yourself: what does this brand do that differentiates it from its competitors – and which is meaningful to the conceptual target?
- Associations that provide the brand with credibility. To determine these, ask yourself: what is it about our product that makes it a credible offering – and in doing so satisfies the customer need (i.e. the critical insight)?
- Associations giving the brand a personality that appeals to its target customers. How is the brand going to be emotionally relevant to the conceptual target?

EXAMPLE

MIKE PALING, FROM PALING WALTERS TARGIS (PWT), IN HIS CONTRIBUTION TO THE BOOK *BRAND MEDICINE* DESCRIBES HOW THE INSIGHT THAT HIS AGENCY HAD INTO WHAT WAS GOING ON IN THE HEARTS AND MINDS OF DOCTORS ENABLED THEM TO BUILD THE ZOFRAN™ BRAND IN THE UNITED KINGDOM INTO ONE WHICH WAS ABLE TO DEFEND ITS SALES REMARKABLY WELL AGAINST THE STRONG COMPETITOR KYTRIL AND OTHER LATER, AND MUCH CHEAPER, ENTRANTS. THE EMOTIONAL RELEVANCE OF ZOFRAN™ WAS THAT IT COULD TAKE CARE OF THE SICKNESS, ALLOWING THE PHYSICIANS AND OTHER HEALTHCARE PROFESSIONALS TO CARE FOR THE PATIENT.

For most brands, in most contexts, it is imperative to develop associations that represent points of parity and points of difference with competitors. Studies of new product introductions have shown that the single best predictor of both new product success and its ability to gain awareness is having a point of difference.

4. Next you need to describe what the brand stands for in its entirety – the core brand values and the brand essence. *To develop the core brand values*, approach as follows:
   (a) List all the words that you believe best describe what the brand is, and what the brand means to the conceptual target.
   (b) Eliminate those descriptions that could arguably be applied equally to one or more of the competitors.
   (c) Now eliminate/refine descriptions on the basis that some of the words used are expressing the same idea, just in a different way.

Eventually you want a list of no more than three words describing what the brand is, and no more than three words describing what the brand means. These 'values' should reflect the brand function, differentiation, reasons to believe and emotional relevance.

For the brand essence, try to describe in a single sentence or using only a few words what the brand stands for. Note there needs to be congruency between all the associations, the brand values and the brand essence.

5. Finally, craft a position statement that is aligned to the strategic objectives and the proposed brand strategy. Ask yourself:
   - Have I described the frame of reference in such a way that it enables customers to immediately understand where to use the product but not in such a way that it will be difficult to broaden its indications or usage elsewhere in the future?
   - Is the benefit that we're promising relevant and compelling? To the physician? To the patient? Is it singular?

- Do the reasons to believe support the benefit and help to differentiate the product from its competitive set?
6. Once you have a position statement that you are satisfied with, you can start working on the key messages (i.e. what it is the customer needs to believe) in order for you to implement your brand strategy.

Guidelines for implementing the brand strategy

So how do we figure out how to express the meaning so that it attaches to the product? You need branding guidance. This guidance is not the same as an execution, nor is it a blueprint. It is a look, a feel, and a sensibility that captures the underlying meaning.

Meaning can be expressed in many ways. It can be expressed verbally through words (and sounds). Or it can be expressed visually through pictures and images. Touch and smell are also possible. In thinking how to express meaning, it is useful to divide the verbal and the visual to give them equal attention and then to distinguish among the major ways of expressing verbal and visual meaning. Such a division shows distinct differences (see Table 6.1 below).

Where brand guidance is provided it can certainly be used as a standard for evaluating all marketing communications. The guidance should define the standard to aspire to in making sure the meaning of the brand is communicated. Figure 6.3 illustrates the hypothetical brand guidance for Zofran™.

TABLE 6.1 EXPRESSING MEANING THROUGH VISUAL AND VERBAL CLUES

Verbal	
Naming	Giving descriptive or figurative names to the product to reflect meaning (e.g. Nurofen)
Wording	Developing a lexicon of words that become a vocabulary having special meaning and that is strongly associated with the brand (e.g. defining a new product class)
Describing	Composing phrases and sentences (slogans) that uniquely capture the brand meaning e.g. Nike 'just do it'
Visual	
Picturing	Illustrating meaning with photographs or drawings or actual things (e.g. type of patient)
Symbolizing	Signifying meaning through more abstract images and graphics, including fonts (e.g. Seretide / Advair flag)
Animating	Conveying meaning by the brand movement and morphing the objects (e.g. the Amoxil brand used the exploding bug to communicate its 'bactericidal action')

FIGURE 6.3   HYPOTHETICAL BRAND GUIDANCE FOR ZOFRAN™. ADAPTED FROM THE BRAND DESIGN APPROACH ADVOCATED IN *KELLOG ON MARKETING*

BRANDING ELEMENTS

Branding elements are those trademarkable devices that serve to identify and differentiate the brand. They will form a part of the branding guidance. The most common branding elements include: the brand name, logo, symbols, slogans, jingles (tunes) and the packaging. The five choice criteria proposed by Kevin L. Keller are summarized in Table 6.2.

Branding elements should be chosen to enhance brand awareness and facilitate the formation of strong, favourable and unique brand associations. The test for any brand element is what people think about the brand if they are exposed to only the element – see Table 6.3.

The entire set of brand elements and associations can be thought of as making up the brand identity. The cohesiveness of the brand identity depends on the extent to which the brand elements and associations are consistent. Because brand elements have different strengths and weaknesses, it is important to 'mix and match' brand elements to maximize their collective contribution to brand equity.

Let us not forget that the way customers and consumers learn about brand meaning is not via a single medium. There is a growing array of media to learn about products. How to market and communicate in an integrated way so that the brand is not lost in all this complexity is the challenge and this is discussed further in Chapters 7 and 13.

TABLE 6.2   BRAND ELEMENT CHOICE CRITERIA

Brand building criteria	Defensive criteria
Memorability:	Transferability:
Easily recognized	Within and across product
Easily recalled	Across geographical boundaries and cultures
Meaningfulness:	Adaptability:
Descriptive	Flexible
Persuasive	Updatable
Fun and interesting	
Rich visual and verbal imagery	
	Protectable:
	Legally
	Competitively

One further issue to keep in mind is that branding is about change. Thus, marketers are forced to ensure that their brand meaning maintains its relevance over time, to find new relevance for their brand. Branding is the act of creative destruction that changes the meaning of relatively more stable products as the lives of customers and consumers change with time. The product itself can stay the same, it is the meaning that it has that is different.

Guidelines for market research

The objective of branding research is to help you identify a conceptual target for your product and then to go on to develop a deep understanding of the conceptual target. For your conceptual target, you need to be able to explain how they view the disease, the products and/or categories of treatment they use to treat the disease, how they feel about their own ability and others' ability to contribute to the management of the disease.

TABLE 6.3   A CHECKLIST FOR ...

The brand name – is it ...

simple and easy to pronounce or spell?

familiar and meaningful i.e. does it tap into existing knowledge structures?

different, distinctive and unusual?

reinforcing some ingredient of the brand position?

A slogan – is it ...

descriptive?

persuasive?

reinforcing the desired brand position and/or point of difference?

The logo and/or symbol – is it ...

distinctive?

embellishing or reinforcing the brand meaning in some way?

well-linked to the brand name?

A jingle – is it ...

consistent with the brand personality?

conveying the brand benefit?

creating an appropriate feeling?

A character – is it ...

colourful and rich in imagery?

communicating a key product benefit?

consistent with the brand personality?

too dominant in relation to the other brand elements?

The package – is it ...

conveying descriptive and persuasive information?

distinctive?

building or reinforcing valuable brand associations?

You're looking for insight into what it is that customers have a definite point of view about, a most deeply held desire, want, hope or fear – that the brand can fulfil.

Frequently asked questions

What are some of the common traps that people fall into?
- Believing that branding is only relevant if you are working in a consumer-led market.
- Believing that global branding is achieved through the brand name and the same picture applied everywhere in the world.
- Poor selection of the focal benefit (often too many). People in our industry always want to say everything about their product. They appear to have great difficulty in distilling out the 'focal benefit'.

- Using normative benefits – i.e. the ones that customers say are important because of societal standards rather then because those benefits actually influence behaviour (for example, nutritional value with foods). Normative benefits are not determinants of brand choice.
- Failure to sustain the brand's position over time. This happens because no one attempted to summarize the brand essence – what the brand really stands for, and its core values.
- The final common mistake is that the basis for differentiation is not viable; that is, it does not connect to a customer need, it's not based on customer insight.

An activity to help you test your skills

Select two markets, one pharma market and one non-pharma market. For each of these markets, choose one brand and then identify two to three other brands competing directly for that same market.

Get samples of the product itself and then either obtain or start looking out for examples of how these brands are being communicated to the market. Identify for each product:

- its frame of reference
- its promise
- the reasons given to believe that promise.

This information may be communicated directly or indirectly, so don't miss some of the subtle clues (for example if an OTC product – which other products is it placed with?).

Now refer to its advertising/communication and decide how they are trying to make this emotionally relevant (meaningful) to the customer? What is the customer insight that underpins this brand's strategy?

Definitions of terms used

- **Brand promise:** This is what the prescriber is going to be able to deliver to his patient or to receive (him/herself) in return for prescribing your product. This benefit can be functional (e.g. powerful relief) or psychological (e.g. enables you to free your patients from their condition).
- **Brand:** The perceptual entity that resides in the mind of the customer and that relates to a product or service.
- **Brand identity:** The key meanings we want associated with the brand. It is the integration of all the key product attributes, as well as the intangible aspects of the brand.
- **Brand function:** The role a particular brand plays in the lives of target customers. We must define what role we want the brand to play to satisfy unmet needs in the market.
- **Brand strategy:** A statement of the intended position of the brand in the customer's mind. It typically includes the target need-state, a description of the conceptual target, the

critical insight, the brand essence, core brand values, a brand position statement and the key messages.

- **Brand values:** Vital elements of the brand that are intrinsic to its existence and cannot be compromised.
- **Branding elements:** Mandatory devices that are used to express/represent and identify the brand. For example: brand name, logo, strap line, typefaces, colours, packaging styles etc. Brand elements provide the hooks to which all brand associations are attached. It is desirable that the **brand elements** have as many of the following characteristics as possible:
  - meaningful (i.e. effectively enable customers to understand the meaning of the brand, e.g. the brand's character)
  - memorable
  - protectable (e.g. legally registerable)
  - adaptable (e.g. can be updated to maintain/enhance memorability, meaningfulness etc.)
  - transferable (e.g. cross-culturally and/or within and across product categories).
- **Conceptual target:** A rich/singular portrait that captures the complete audience of the brand. A 'natural' grouping of customers, bound by a common set of values, singular outlook, attitudes and aspirations. A single access point for our communication.
- **Critical insight:** The most deeply held desire, want, hope or fear of the conceptual target that the brand can best fulfil.
- **Emotional insights:** Qualitative research designed to probe the customer's subconscious to discover deeply rooted feelings about a disease, the available treatments and the available brands.
- **Frame of reference:** The people for whom your product should be prescribed, or the situation or circumstances under which it should be prescribed.
- **Positioning:** The positive and negative associations that are perceived to be related to a product.
- **Product position statement:** A clear statement of:
  - frame of reference
  - compelling argument (promise) and
  - the evidence for that argument (reasons to believe the promise)
  - occasionally a higher level benefit.
- **Reasons to believe:** One of the most critical pieces of a brand position statement. It must clearly tell the prescriber why or how your product can deliver the benefit you are claiming, and the rationale must make sense.

Recommended reading

Aaker, David A. (1991) *Managing Brand Equity*, USA: MacMillan Inc.

Aaker, David A. (1996) *Building Strong Brands*, New York, USA: The Free Press.

Aaker, David A. (2000) *Brand Leadership*, New York, USA: The Free Press.

Blackett, T. and Robins, D. (2001) *Brand Medicine: The role of branding in the Pharmaceutical Industry*, Hampshire: Palgrave Publishers Ltd.

Gobe, Marc (2001) *Emotional Branding*, Oxford: Windsor Books Ltd.

Iacobucci, D. (2001) *Kellog on Marketing*, Canada: John Wiley & Sons.

Interbrand Healthcare (2001) *Brand Medicine. The role of branding in the pharmaceutical industry*, Hampshire, England: Palgrave.

Keller, Kevin L. (1998) *Strategic Brand Management. Building, Measuring, and Managing Brand Equity*, New Jersey, USA: Prentice Hall.

Mann, C.C. and Plummer, M.L. (1991) *The Aspirin Wars. Money, Medicine and 100 years of Rampant Competition*, Boston, Massachusetts: Harvard Business School Press.

Ries, A. and Trout, J. (1986) *Positioning: The Battle for Your Mind*, Singapore: McGraw-Hill International Editions.

Schulz, E. (2000) *The Marketing Game: How the world's best companies play to win*, London: Kogan Page Ltd.

7

Completing the Plan

In this chapter we will consider:

- How does the pre-launch plan differ from a typical brand plan?
- What are the key components of a pre-launch brand plan?
- How does the need to deliver integrated marketing communications affect the way we approach pre-launch planning?
- How to approach the development of the pre-launch brand plan
- Frequently asked questions
- An activity to help you test your skills
- Definitions of terms used
- Recommended reading.

How does the pre-launch plan differ from a typical brand plan?

Following the completion of the external and internal analysis (the situational analysis), you have a good understanding of the market in which you are going to compete and also a good understanding of your current competitive position.

Through your strategic objectives and your brand strategy you have set out what you are trying to achieve by the time you are ready to launch. Now you need to decide how you are going to make this happen. The pre-launch plan is the document that summarizes the range of tactics that need to be implemented in order to ensure that you are where you need to be at the time of launch.

The value drivers in the 'pre-launch' phase are:

- strategy and planning
- researching the market
- preparing the market
- preparing the company
- capturing product value (regulatory and reimbursement strategies) and
- life cycle management.

What are the key components of a pre-launch plan?

CRITICAL SUCCESS FACTORS

These are those elements (within your control) which define the priorities for future market success. Focusing on them will ensure that you progress from your current situation to realize your strategic objectives and brand position. These critical elements will include two or three critical brand triggers and the priority success factors. The critical success factors facilitate the co-ordination of the various groups working to implement the pre-launch strategy. It is generally agreed that you might have up to five critical success factors (CSFs). No more!

NON-FINANCIAL OBJECTIVES

Non-financial objectives are statements of what is to be accomplished in relation to each CSF, by the overall marketing programme, pre-launch. They are usually defined in terms of specific measurable outcomes. Good non-financial objectives are quantifiable; they delineate the target market and note the timeframe for accomplishment. To be effective, non-financial objectives must be realistic and attainable.

Typically you will have only one or two outcomes (or objectives) in relation to each critical success factor. You will often have secondary objectives that are related to actions that you must take to solve specific issues and thus achieve your primary objective. Do not confuse these with the primary non-financial objective.

Many people have difficulty with this most critical step in the marketing planning process – setting realistic objectives that will guide the development of the pre-launch plan. While the task of setting objectives can be complex and difficult, it must be done properly because specific goals and objectives are the foundation on which all programme and budgeting decisions are made.

MARKETING PROGRAMME

The primary input to building brand equity comes from marketing activities related to the brand and the day-to-day actions of everyone in contact with the customer. These marketing activities are referred to as the marketing programme and this should be designed in the context of the critical success factors and the associated non-financial objectives. The marketing mix is essentially a conceptual framework, which has been developed to help structure the approach to the marketing programme. There are many different approaches to the marketing mix, e.g. 4Ps, 5Ps, 7Ps etc. They could all be argued to have their limitations, which is why I'm keen that we understand the key principle underpinning the marketing mix: that there are a number of building blocks that form the basis of any marketing programme, and that all these variables communicate something about the brand, which is why they need careful consideration.

Below I discuss the 4Ps as a basic and practical framework and explore application to the pharmaceutical industry.

THE FOUR Ps

- **Product strategy:** The product itself is at the heart of brand equity, as it is the primary influence of what the consumers and customers (through patient feedback) experience with a brand. A lot of the communications are also product-centric. For a global marketing team, product strategy is likely to include all activities relating to the clinical development and product development that form the life cycle management plan. For local operating companies, you should consider 'local' clinical trial programmes that might add value to the product experience.
- **Price strategy:** Think of this as the 'capturing value' activity required to get the product registered, reimbursed and on to local formularies. This typically involves activities around pricing and health economics.
- **Place strategy:** The number of countries in which the product is available (its place status) and the manner by which the product becomes available (its reimbursement status) can have a profound impact on the resulting equity and ultimate sales success of a brand. Think of this as the design and management of the regulatory strategy from a global marketing standpoint and the design and management of the access strategy from a local standpoint.
- **Promotion strategy:** Your marketing communications are perhaps the most flexible element of the marketing mix. Marketing communications are the means by which you attempt to inform, persuade and remind your consumers and customers, directly or indirectly, about the brands you sell.

  Marketing communications are the 'voice' of the brand and are a means by which it can establish a dialogue and build relationships with consumers and customers. There are wide ranges of vehicles today that you can use to convey your communications (see Figure 7.1).

A MECHANISM FOR MONITORING AND CONTROL

A series of measurements need to be agreed and then actioned to make sure that the pre-launch plan is implemented. These measurements will cover aspects such as some of the key programmes, through to the attitudes and beliefs and levels of awareness that we intend to have in place before we get to market. This is another important reason for setting specific non-financial objectives as they provide a benchmark against which the success or failure of the pre-launch plan can be monitored. Without specific objectives, it is extremely difficult to determine what the marketing programme efforts accomplished.

How does the need to deliver integrated marketing communications affect the way we approach pre-launch planning?

The first point is that integrated marketing communications (IMC) requires the recognition of all contact points where the customer may encounter the company, its products and its brands. Each contact point delivers a message – good, bad or indifferent. You should be striving to deliver a consistent and positive message at all contact points.

The second point is that you should be using the multiplicity of contact points available to you – not put all your money behind one medium. This argues for thinking creatively about which tools you might use

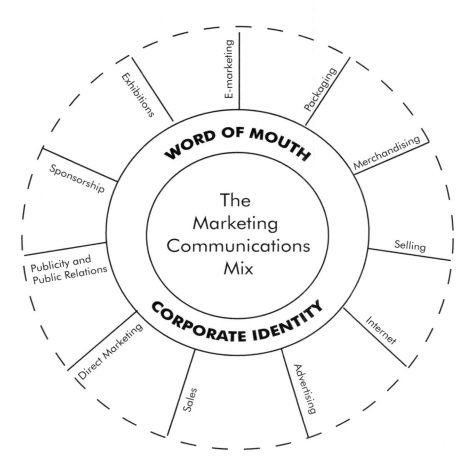

FIGURE 7.1   THE MARKETING COMMUNICATIONS MIX. SOURCE: P. R. SMITH AND J. TAYLOR (2004) *MARKETING COMMUNICATIONS*, 4TH EDN, LONDON: KOGAN PAGE

EXAMPLE

BRISTOL-MYERS-SQUIBB WON THE BID TO DEVELOP TAXOL IN 1991. BMS SAW IN TAXOL THE OPPORTUNITY TO BECOME A DOMINANT PLAYER IN THE ONCOLOGY ARENA. CANCER WAS CONSIDERED A DEATH SENTENCE IN 1991. SINCE FEW CANCERS WERE CURABLE, ONCOLOGISTS WERE GIVEN TO EXPERIMENTATION WITH DOSING REGIMENS AND PRODUCT COMBINATIONS AND HAD A RELATIVELY HIGH COMFORT LEVEL WITH THE OFF-LABEL USE OF ONCOLYTICS IN THEIR ATTEMPTS TO SAVE PATIENTS' LIVES.

PROMOTION

BY THE TIME THEY WERE READY TO LAUNCH IN 1992, BMS HAD ESTABLISHED EXCELLENT CONNECTIONS WITH OPINION LEADERS AND SPEAKERS. ONCOLOGISTS WERE EAGER FOR THE PRODUCT, CONVINCED IT WAS INNOVATIVE AND ALREADY HAD A LOT OF EXPERIENCE USING THE PRODUCT. THIS HAD BEEN ACCOMPLISHED THROUGH THE USE OF PROFESSIONAL AND PUBLIC RELATIONS, EXTENSIVE MEDICAL EDUCATION AND ENSURING THAT THE PRODUCT WAS STUDIED AS MUCH AS POSSIBLE PRE-LAUNCH. THROUGHOUT THE WHOLE DEVELOPMENT PROCESS, THE KEY MESSAGES ABOUT TAXOL WERE AROUND 'EXCITING NEW DATA' AND 'TAXOL COMING SOON'.

PRODUCT

IT APPEARS THAT THE CLINICAL TRIAL DEPARTMENT WAS CLOSELY IN TUNE WITH THE MARKETING STRATEGY FOR TAXOL. INVESTIGATORS STUDYING TAXOL STUDIED IT THE WAY BMS WANTED IT STUDIED, SO THAT AT LAUNCH, ALL THE PUBLISHED STUDIES

WERE CONSISTENT WITH STRATEGY AND DID NOT CONFUSE THE MARKET PLACE. PUBLICATIONS AND EXPERIENCE TRIALS WERE ONE OF THE KEY VEHICLES USED FOR IMPLEMENTING THE MARKETING STRATEGY.

THROUGH THIS INTENSIVE RESEARCH AND PUBLICATION STRATEGY, TAXOL MANAGED ITS PRODUCT LIFE CYCLE. THE PRODUCT WAS TECHNICALLY LAUNCHED WITH A SECOND-LINE OVARIAN CANCER INDICATION IN 1992. THIS WAS FOLLOWED WITH SECOND LINE IN BREAST CANCER, FIRST LINE IN OVARIAN CANCER IN 1996, NSCL (NON-SMALL CELL LUNG CANCER) IN 1998 ETC.

TAXOL WAS ORIGINALLY LAUNCHED AS A 24-HOUR INFUSION WHICH REQUIRED HOSPITALIZATION. IN 1993, BMS CAME OUT WITH A 3-HOUR INFUSION WHICH ALLOWED THE PRODUCT TO BE GIVEN IN THE ONCOLOGIST'S OFFICE/OUTPATIENT DEPARTMENT. THE 3-HOUR INFUSION ALSO CAME WITH SUBSTANTIAL PATENT PROTECTION.

PRICE

BMS BUILT A STATE OF THE ART REIMBURSEMENT SUPPORT CENTRE FOR PATIENTS AND PHYSICIANS TO EXPEDITE TREATMENT APPROVAL AND PAYMENT IN THE USA.

PLACE

IN THE US, BMS RESPONDED TO THE PHYSICIAN NEEDS ARISING OUT OF THE GROWING PRACTICE OF ADMINISTERING INJECTABLE ONCOLYTICS IN THE OFFICE. THEY ENTERED INTO A JOINT VENTURE WITH AXION FOR DELIVERY OF ALL BMS ONCOLOGY PRODUCTS DIRECTLY TO THE PHYSICIAN'S OFFICE.

> The third and final point is that not only should your different promotion/education activities be integrated; all four Ps must be integrated. For example, the company cannot intend to charge a high price for its product but provide little in the way of data to support the high price.

> The great interdependencies among marketing elements require the most careful planning.

How to approach the development of the pre-launch plan

1. The most important step in the development of the pre-launch marketing plan is deciding what is going to be critical to success, given where you need to be, at the time of launch. These critical success factors along with the non-financial objectives provide the structure for the pre-launch plan.

   You have already considered which issues and/or opportunities you are going to take advantage of as part of your strategy formulation, and brand strategy decision process. Now you need to formally consider which strengths and/or weaknesses you need to leverage to implement this strategy.

   If you are working on the global marketing team, then your primary responsibility is in identifying the two or three critical brand triggers (applicable globally) and two or three success factors that need to be leveraged in order for the entire company to be in a strong position to implement the brand strategy.

   Each local operating company should be crystal clear about the local issues and opportunities that need to be managed up to launch and use this local insight and understanding to independently define what the local CSFs are. They should include the – centrally defined – two or three critical brand triggers.

2. As soon as you are satisfied that you are clear on the pre-launch business priorities (i.e. the CSFs), you need to set objectives. Start with one critical success factor at a time. I find the Millward Brown 'BrandDynamics™ Pyramid' (see Figure 7.2) extremely helpful to the objective-setting process. Let me explain both the model and how I use it.

This BrandDynamics™ Pyramid is used by Millward Brown to measure brand equity. It explains the strength of the relationship that customers have with the brand and allows one to identify which areas of marketing activity it makes most sense to focus on.

The way I use it to help me with the objective-setting process is as follows. I take each CSF and decide which area on the pyramid this CSF is going to contribute to. I allow myself up to two areas for any one CSF. In this way I make sure that, through my CSFs, I am managing the entire brand building process. As soon as I have decided the role each CSF needs to play in the brand building process, I am in a much better position to set appropriate objectives.

EXAMPLE

IMAGINE THAT I AM RESPONSIBLE FOR THE PRE-LAUNCH MARKETING OF VIAGRA (THE IMPOTENCE MEDICATION). LET'S SAY THAT ONE OF MY PRE-LAUNCH CRITICAL SUCCESS FACTORS IS ENSURING THAT WE HAVE AN 'ACCEPTABLE FORMULATION' BECAUSE I KNOW THAT AT THE MOMENT THIS IS ONE OF THE MAIN REASONS THAT PEOPLE DON'T GET TREATED.

IF I LINK THIS TO THE BRANDDYNAMICS™ PYRAMID, IT WILL CREATE 'RELEVANCE' AND I'M GOING TO SUGGEST ALSO 'ADVANTAGE'. THUS I'VE SELECTED TWO AREAS OF THE PYRAMID WHICH THIS CSF IMPACTS.

SO HOW DOES THIS HELP ME WRITING THE OBJECTIVES? WELL WITH 'RELEVANCE', WHAT I'M ACTUALLY GOING TO DO IS SET AN OBJECTIVE WITH REGARD TO THE PERCENTAGE OF PEOPLE WHO MIGHT SEEK TREATMENT WHEN AN 'ACCEPTABLE TREATMENT SOLUTION' IS AVAILABLE.

THEN I WOULD WRITE A SECOND OBJECTIVE AGAINST 'CREATE ADVANTAGE.' THIS OBJECTIVE WILL RELATE TO PHYSICIAN PREFERENCE TO PRESCRIBE OUR FORMULATION.

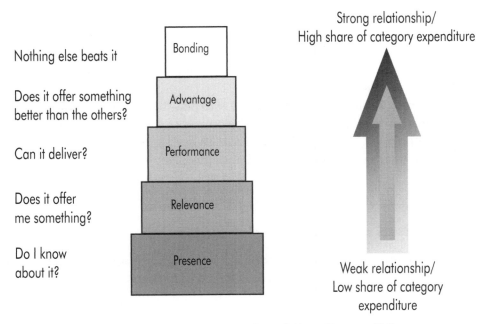

FIGURE 7.2 BRAND DYNAMICS PYRAMID. SOURCE: MILLWARD BROWN'S BRANDDYNAMICS™ PYRAMID

3. Once you have set your objectives, you will be faced with a number of strategic and tactical options. Your choice should be determined according to how well a particular option satisfies the non-financial objective.

4. Before you start planning in detail for each non-financial objective, you should describe your overall approach to the marketing programme by thinking specifically around how you are going to ensure that each aspect of the marketing mix is integrated and supports the brand strategy.

5. Next, flesh out in detail the tactics that need to be undertaken. Focus on the objectives one at a time and ask yourself how you are going to go about achieving that objective. List the relevant tactics against each objective.

6. To ensure that you have thought through all aspects of the marketing programme, you might find it useful to apply the checklist below:

   (a) Have I captured all the pre-clinical and clinical work that needs to take place pre-launch? Can I support this requirement by linking it back to one or more of the non-financial objectives?

   (b) What about the product's development, e.g. which indications we get to market with and which follow? Which formulations do we have at launch and which follow? Delivery systems etc. Am I clear about what it is absolutely necessary to have to meet our objectives and what might be a 'nice to have'?

   (c) Am I confident that we have identified all the things that we need to do to get the product registered, reimbursed and on to local formularies?

   (d) With regard to our proposed pre-launch educational activity, are we confident that:

      i)   the programme will ensure that sufficient people are exposed to the appropriate communication?

      ii) there are sufficient opportunities for the right people to see or be exposed to our communication?

      iii) we have planned our communication activity in an cost-efficient way?

      iv) the vehicles we are using will break through the clutter (i.e. ensure our communication has impact)?

      v)   the vehicles we are using support and reinforce our brand strategy?

      vi) the receiver of the communication will be motivated to change his/her attitude and/or belief and/or action?

   For both the global marketing teams and local marketing teams, pre-launch marketing communications would include educational activities that 'prepare the market' as well as prepare the company.

7. Now cost out the tactics. Are you satisfied that you are spending enough and doing enough to achieve your non-financial objectives? If you are satisfied with the answer to this question, you can now shift your focus to set up mechanisms for monitoring and controlling progress against implementation of this plan.

Frequently asked questions

- **How many non-financial objectives might be appropriate?** My preference is to maintain the concept of 'focus', which means, at the most, two non-financial objectives against each critical success factor. This does not preclude you from having a number of milestones below each objective, but it encourages you to be clear about precisely what it is that you are setting out to achieve through each CSF.

● **A lot of my planned activities can apply to more than one objective. How do I avoid this repetition?** My view is that you should be very clear about the objective of each activity – this requires discipline and requires you to think about the objective first and then only decide on which tactics.

I always find it fascinating that when I try to encourage people to be single-minded as to which objective any one tactic is fulfilling, there is a lot of resistance – I suspect because very often we are doing things and we are not quite sure why we are doing them, i.e. we are hoping by throwing a lot of money at the situation ... something will work.

An activity to help you test your skills

1. List all the pre-marketing tools that your business unit is currently using. Which are the most important? How are you deciding this? Are any tools missing from this list? Why would you say that? Are any tools in the list a waste of money? Can you sort the tools into their roles (i.e. align them to your non-financial objectives)?

2. Are you satisfied with the proportion of funds that you are spending on each promotional tool? Against each non-financial objective? If you were going to shift funds, which tools would you reduce and which would you increase? Would you shift the balance of funds allocated to achieving the different non-financial objectives?

Definitions of terms used

● **Critical success factors (CSFs):** The critical success factors are the most important conditions that a business must identify and satisfy if it is to be an effective competitor and thrive. They are not objectives in themselves, but they are the factors that play a major role in guiding the company towards business success.

● **Implementation plan:** Specifies the tactics and activities that need to be undertaken to implement the strategy. The implementation plan should clearly define:
  — which non-financial objective(s) will be addressed
  — what tactics are going to be implemented in order to meet the non-financial objectives
  — what action is to be taken
  — priority of action
  — who is responsible for the action
  — how much of which resources (money, headcount, time etc.) will be used
  — when the action is to be started and completed
  — how and when the success/effectiveness of *top* priority actions will be evaluated.

● **Key tactics:** A set of tactics that will need to be undertaken in order to support the implementation of a strategy.

● **Key measures of success:** A component of a marketing plan that reports progress towards achievement.

● **Marketing programme:** Consists of the marketing activities that are undertaken to build brand equity. They cover activities relating to all elements of the 'marketing mix'.

- **Non-financial objectives:** The expression of success regarding critical success factors:
  - Specific
  - Measurable
  - Ambitious
  - Realistic, and
  - Time-limited.
- **Monitoring and control:** A process involving review and correction of target objectives, target dates, and target tactics and actions against what actually happened.

Recommended reading

Keller, Kevin L. (1998) *Strategic Brand Management. Building, Measuring, and Managing Brand Equity*, New Jersey, USA: Prentice Hall.

Kotler, P. (1999) *Kotler on Marketing: How to create, win and dominate markets*, Great Britain: Simon & Schuster.

Smith, P.R., Berry, C. and Pulford, A. (2000) *Strategic Marketing Communications: new ways to build and integrate communications*, London: Kogan Page.

Smith, P.R. with Taylor, J. (2004) *Marketing Communications* (4th edition), London: Kogan Page.

Part II

Planning for an In-line Brand

Reviewing the Market Size, Value and Competitor Dynamics

In this chapter we will consider:

- What is it that we are trying to understand?
- What are the deliverables from this analysis?
- What thinking frameworks facilitate this review?
- How you should approach the review
- Maximizing the utility of market research
- Frequently asked questions
- An activity that you might undertake to help you improve your skill at reviewing the size of the market
- Definitions of terms used
- Recommended reading.

What is it that we are trying to understand?

With an in-line product, the focus is on the target need-state and/or patient segment(s). The following questions need to be answered for the 'target patient segment(s)' and for the market overall:

1. Is the treated population growing or declining? And by how much? Is this in line with what we expected? If not, is the difference significant?
2. What has contributed to the growth or decline? For example, if the treated population is growing, could it be because more patients are diagnosed and consequently treated? Or could it be because physicians are writing more prescriptions etc? Are the assumptions that we made holding true? If not, what needs adjusting?
3. Is the pattern of what is happening to patients (in terms of getting into the healthcare system, getting diagnosed, getting a Rx, a particular therapy class and/or brand) different from what we assumed? If so, how so?
4. Has the value of what the patient is worth changed at all? For example, has there been an increase/decrease in treatment length? What about changes to the cost/day of treating these patients?
5. Which brands are the winners, which brands are the losers? Is this in line with what we expected?

What are the deliverables from this analysis?

After having completed this analysis you will have an appreciation of: the current and anticipated future size of the target patient segment(s) and the market overall; the current and anticipated future value of the target patient segment(s); and the total market value. This serves as the basis for your forecast which we discuss in Chapter 12.

What thinking frameworks facilitate this review?

- **The patient flow analysis:** So what does a patient flow analysis look like? The structure of the patient flow may well vary according to the therapeutic area. Essentially, one is interested in identifying the key decision points that affect what happens to the patient from the point at which the condition manifests itself, through to the point that they receive drug treatment. Figure 8.1a illustrates an example of a patient flow, for patients with persistent asthma (a segment of the asthma market). This is contrasted with a patient flow diagram for someone with chronic heart failure who has also previously suffered from a myocardial infarction (a segment of the CHF market) (see Figure 8.1b).
- **Competitor analysis:** Because of the way you are approaching this analysis, when it comes to competition, the intent is to understand/identify the specific Rx products that your product will be competing with, given your target patient segment(s) and the different patient populations that are embraced by the target patient segment(s). There is a need to understand how these products are performing, i.e. what share of the patient opportunity they have and what share of the market value they have.

  Indirect competitors will be managed as threats to the potential (if they satisfy an unmet need). They will not be included when trying to 'value the actual market'.
- **The key trends analysis:** This analysis is necessary to ensure that your forecast is based on both the shape and nature of the market today as well as how this might change in the

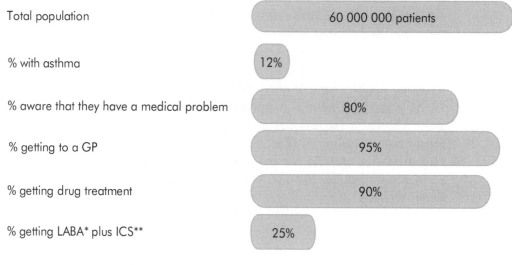

Total population — 60 000 000 patients

% with asthma — 12%

% aware that they have a medical problem — 80%

% getting to a GP — 95%

% getting drug treatment — 90%

% getting LABA* plus ICS** — 25%

* LABA (Long acting bronchodilator)

** ICS (inhaled corticosteroid)

FIGURE 8.1A   PATIENT FLOW DIAGRAM FOR SOMEONE WITH PERSISTENT ASTHMA. LABA, LONG ACTING BRONCHODILATOR; ICS, INHALED CORTICOSTEROID

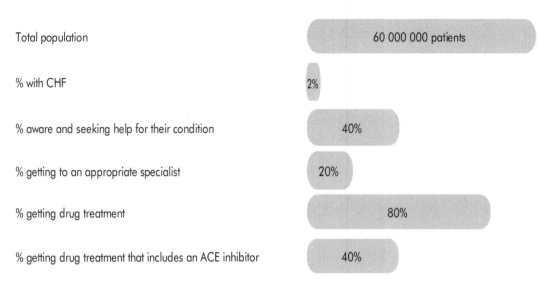

FIGURE 8.1B   PATIENT FLOW DIAGRAM FOR SOMEONE WITH CHF (PREVIOUSLY HAD AN MI)

future. You typically complete a key trends analysis only after you are convinced that you have a good understanding of the market *as it exists today*.

The quality of thought, debate and discussion that is put into the interpretation of the future is very important, and makes this analysis worthwhile.

When considering the future there is an awful lot that could be different and probably an equal amount that could be the same. The challenge is to identify those factors that are going to significantly change the shape and/or nature of the future market. In this way you can make an informed decision as to how to adjust the underlying trend. The focus is on events taking place that are independent of your own strategy.

With the future there are no facts. At best you have a high degree of certainty (a) that an event will take place and (b) about the implication of that event on your target patient segment. Events that have both a high impact and are associated with a high degree of certainty are referred to as key trends. In some cases it is likely that the event itself or the implication of the event is surrounded by a degree of uncertainty – these events will be referred to as critical uncertainties.

The future market size and value is predicted based on these key trends. Critical uncertainties can be fed into upside and downside forecasts.

How you should approach the review

1. Use a similar structure to that embodied in Table 8.1.
2. Describe the different patient sub-groups that are relevant, given the 'need' that you are targeting: treat these as segments.
3. Update the patient numbers for each segment.
   - If you don't already have one, develop a structure for the patient flow. This structure needs to be one that can be applied to the target patient segment(s) as well as to the market as a whole. This requires that you understand the significant decision areas that influence what happens to the patient, from the point at which the condition manifests

TABLE 8.1 UNDERLYING TREND FORECAST

	Yr − 3	Yr − 2	Yr − 1	Current	Yr + 1	Yr + 2	Yr + 3	Yr + 4	Yr + 5
Population Prevalence % Incidence % Total population PER SEGMENT % Diagnosed % Treated % Treated by relevant therapeutic class									
Numbers treated with the relevant therapeutic class									
Cost per day Average number of days treated									
Market/segment value									

Key trends	What do they impact?	When?				
		Yr + 1	Yr + 2	Yr + 3	Yr + 4	Yr + 5
Trend a Trend b Trend c etc.	% diagnosed % treated by relevant therapeutic class no impact					

| Revised numbers …
Treated with the relevant
therapeutic class | | | | | | | | | |
| Revised market/ segment
value | | | | | | | | | |

itself, to the point at which the patient receives treatment. It is the same approach that is taken when building an epidemiology-based forecasting model. You might find the following questions helpful:
— Are people seeking treatment?
— Do they get to a physician?
— Is their condition easy to recognize?
— Do they get medication?
— Do they get the 'appropriate' medication?
- Now focus on the facts:
  — Has the total potential population increased/decreased? Enter the latest data (see Table 8.1).
  — For each segment (patient sub-group): has any aspect of what is happening to the patient changed – for example, are more people seeking treatment, getting diagnosed, getting a prescription etc? Enter the latest data (see Table 8.1).
- Now shift your focus to the future (the implications of your key trends analysis) – see Table 8.1
  - Are there new events or trends that could affect the future 'size' of the market? If yes, make a note of what they are and refine your estimate of the future size of the market (see Figure 8.2).
4 Update the segment value.
  - For each segment (patient sub-group), identify whom you are competing with for that prescription. Who are the relevant competitors? How many should be included? Which ones should be considered? You're best answering these questions by talking to customers.
    (a) Give a group of customers a description of the segments (patient sub-groups). Ask them which products they most often use in each situation.
    (b) A second group of customers can be given a list of products and asked how likely they are to use the product, given each segment (patient sub-group).
    (c) Define your competitive set based on their perceived appropriateness for the segments (patient sub-groups).
  - Once you have listed whom you are competing with, gather the sales data for these products. Where the product is used in more than one segment, you need to consider how their sales data might be apportioned to the relevant segments in order for you to be able to determine a realistic value for each segment (see Table 8.2).

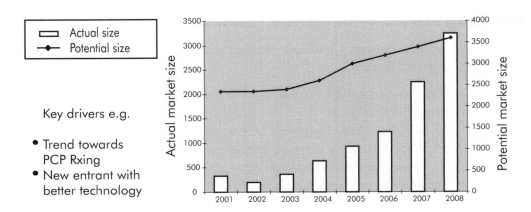

FIGURE 8.2 KEY MARKET DRIVERS AND THEIR IMPACT ON THE MARKET SIZE (POTENTIAL AND ACTUAL)

TABLE 8.2   ASSIGNING A VALUE TO THE DIFFERENT MARKET SEGMENTS

List of brands [total value]			
Brand A [$100m]	$80m	$10m	$10m
Brand B [$500m]	—	$500m	—
Brand C [$800m]	—	$700m	$100
Brand D [$900m]	$100m	$200m	$600m

- Now, focus on the facts:
  - What is the latest sales data that you have for these competitors? Enter the data. How has this affected the total market and target segment value (is it increasing/decreasing)?
- Next, think about the future (the implications of your key trends analysis) see Table 8.3.
  - Are there new events or trends that could affect the future 'value' of the market? If yes, make a note of what they are and refine your estimate of the future market value (see Figure 8.3).
5. Update competitor market shares (competitor analysis).
  - Once again – start by focusing on the facts:
    - How have the competitors been performing? Are they increasing or decreasing their share of the available patients? Enter the data.
    - Note you should only forecast the future shares for each of the competitors when you are addressing your own sales forecast. This is because your strategy might well influence that forecast (see Figure 8.4).
6. Finally, reflect on the market dynamics: do you need to make any adjustments to your thinking on what proportion of the market is 'available' or represents an opportunity? This number is typically calculated from new, switch and/or add-on therapies as appropriate. Does the size of the 'available' market vary across segments?

Maximizing the utility of market research

The challenge here is utilizing the data that is available to review the size, trends etc. A few guidelines follow:

- The *potential* of the target need-state is all about sizing how big it could be. There are two considerations here:
  (a) Which patient sub-groups (segments)?
  (b) What can realistically be considered to be potential? Those seeking treatment? Or those diagnosed? Or those getting a prescription?
  The answers to these questions will vary according to the market and the product that you are planning for. Make sure that the potential you are planning for is realistic.

TABLE 8.3 Revised Value Forecast

	Yr − 3	Yr − 2	Yr − 1	Current	Yr + 1	% Growth	Yr + 2	% Growth	Yr + 3	% Growth	Yr + 4	% Growth
Underlying trend												
Revised numbers.... treated with the relevant therapeutic class (key trends analysis)												
Revised average treatment value per patient/per patient opportunity												
Revised market/ segment value												
Assumptions												

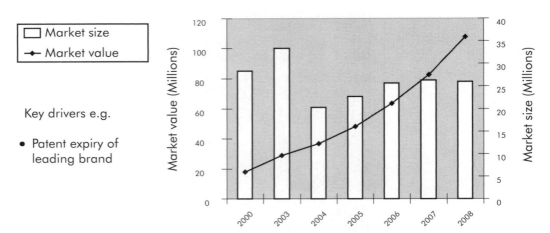

FIGURE 8.3   KEY MARKET DRIVERS AND THEIR IMPACT ON THE MARKET SIZE AND MARKET VALUE

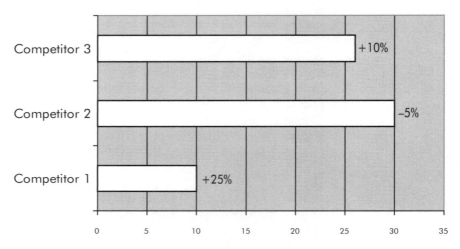

FIGURE 8.4   COMPETITOR MARKET SHARES AND GROWTH

- The **actual** size of the target need-state is the number of people treated by Rx today across the different patient segments (patient sub-groups). The 'actual' size of each segment (patient sub-group) one would expect to be different in different countries, and for different reasons.

Frequently asked questions

- The data provided is typically available for the market and for certain classes of products, occasionally by diagnosis but rarely by 'segment'. How should we manage, given this situation? You're best answering these questions by talking to customers.
  (a) Give a group of customers a description of the target need-state and relevant patient segments. Ask them which products they most often use in this situation.

(b) A second group of customers can be given a list of products and asked how likely they are to use the product, given the need-state and different patient segments.

(c) Define your competitive set based on their perceived appropriateness for the target need-state and relevant patient segments.

- **How do we know how well competitors are doing in each patient segment if we don't have data for competitor products cut this way?** Once again, you're best answering these questions by talking to customers and trying to understand how they view the competitor products and their usage of them in the context of the target need-state and patient segments. You will have hard data which gives you the big picture for the competitor, i.e. overall, are its sales growing or declining? You then need to take the insight you have as to where their sales are coming from and apply this to the hard data. Remember; the actual data itself does not tell us anything – we are trying to make sure that we understand whether they are more or less successful than we are at satisfying each of the segment's needs.

- **How can we quantify the patient flow when this data is not available to us and the cost of going out and obtaining this data is prohibitive?** You should feel comfortable with estimating the percentage of patients moving from one point in the patient flow to another. Note that there is some data which is 'hard' data – for example, disease prevalence (although I accept that when you go to different data sources this might vary significantly too). Probably the most important point to remember is that whatever number you put in, it is never going to be precisely right. What we are striving to achieve in this situation is for the number to be the right order of magnitude rather than precise.

An activity that you might undertake to help you improve your skill at reviewing the size of the market

Completing this exercise should demonstrate to you that even if you do not have data, you can make an informed guess as to the potential size and patient flow for any one segment.

Let us assume that there are two segments in the hypertension market – the first is 'to reduce the blood pressure' and the second is 'to prevent cardiovascular disease'.

Which of the following patient types could fall into which segments?

- a person over 65
- a pregnant woman
- a 40-year-old professional male.

Let us say that each segment starts with a potential of 100 people. Where will the differences in the patient flow lie? And how significant would these differences be? Over time, which segments will have seen the greatest change and why?

- Numbers getting into the healthcare system?
- Numbers treated with a prescription med?
- Numbers treated with an ACE inhibitor?

If you explain your thinking to someone else, does your rationale stand up when challenged? If it does, you're good to go!

Definitions of terms used

- **Competition:** This includes any company which provides or will be in a position to offer a product/service or solution that meets the customer's needs.
- **Decision phases:** The key steps that determine what happens to the patient: whether they get into the healthcare system and what happens to them once they are in the system.
- **Key trends:** Those trends and/or changes whose impact on the future shape or nature of the market is thought to be high, and where the likelihood of them happening is also high.
- **Market research:** Information used to identify and define marketing opportunities and challenges; generate and refine marketing actions; monitor marketing performance; and improve the understanding of marketing as a process.
- **Market value:** The total sales value of competing products in a given market.
- **Market volume:** The total number of 'available' patients or patient opportunities in a given market.
- **Patient flow:** This is a thinking framework used to assess the market in terms of the size of the patient population, whether the market and/or target patient segment are growing, and what is contributing to that growth, i.e. how many patients are getting into the healthcare system, how many are diagnosed or recognized as having the disease, how many are receiving drug therapy etc. It is also used to determine the strategic issues which are resulting in the gap between the 'true' patient potential and the actual size of the market.
- **Potential:** The amount of business that might be realized in the market if the total population who could benefit from the therapeutic approach had access to the treatment.
- **Target need-state:** The treatment goal that we are feeding/reinforcing and by definition the patient population that is embraced by this treatment goal.
- **Trends:** Identified or forecast patterns of change over time.

Recommended reading

Dogramatzis, Dimitris (2001) *Pharmaceutical Marketing: A practical guide*, Denver, Colorado: IHS Health Group.

Kotler, P. (1988) *Marketing Management: Analysis, Planning, Implementation and Control* (6th edition), New Jersey, USA: Prentice-Hall International.

9

Reviewing the Brand Situation

In this chapter we will consider:

- What is it that we are trying to understand?
- What is the deliverable?
- What are the challenges?
- How to approach the review
- Maximizing the utility of market research
- Frequently asked questions
- An activity that you might undertake to help you improve your skill at reviewing the brand situation
- Definitions of terms used
- Recommended reading.

What is it that we are trying to understand?

Strengthening and improving, for the target need-state and/or patient segment(s), one's understanding of:

- **The opportunities and threats:** The description of opportunities and threats needs to reflect the company's latest and best understanding of each of the segments (patient subgroups) today and how this might change in the future. Improved understanding must exist. You have at least a year's extra experience as a result of actively operating in this market. Someone will have learnt something that you did not fully understand or appreciate when you developed the plan last year.

You should be particularly keen to identify what has been learnt about:

1. customer attitudes and beliefs that represent an opportunity or a threat (a barrier), and
2. future events that could affect whether each of the segments (patient sub-groups) become more or less attractive in the future.

- **The company's competitive position (i.e. strengths and weaknesses):** The decisions that you take for an established brand are complicated by the set of associations already in place. This means that you must understand where you are *today* with regard to the following:
  - what customers strongly associate with your brand
  - how these associations work for you (strengths) or how they work against you (weaknesses)
  - whether your brand image is fragmented or consistent.

You also need to understand this same information for your competitors. Figures 9.1a and 9.1b provide an example of how the SWOT analysis was strengthened or improved for a product in a specialist market, one year on.

Opportunities

- Current treatments not controlling the problem
- The alternative drug class used causes problems
- Unmet need
- Decline in use of alternative drug class due to mortality data
- Increase in provision of dialysis centres
- Decline in use of our direct competitor due to availability of effective alternatives
- Reduction in target levels

Threats

- Increase in use of nocturnal/other improved techniques
- 2nd in class

Strengths

- Education
- KOL relationships
- Strength of binding
- Low pill burden
- Chewable tablets
- Best data

Weaknesses

- Not perceived as powerful
- Safety concerns
- No comparative cost-benefit

FIGURE 9.1A   SWOT BEFORE THE STRATEGIC REVIEW

Opportunities

- Patients need an effective agent
- There is a decline in physician comfort with using high doses of the alternative to this drug class
- Recommended target levels are being reduced
- Recognition of benefits to early treatment
- Significant use of the direct competitor despite physician concerns, due to lack of alternatives
- Perception that the latest competitor product in this market hasn't met efficacy expectations

Threats

- The number of these patients will shrink as the drug causing the problem is used less
- Inappropriate dosing and/or poor patient compliance result in poor efficacy
- Niching activities by the competitors
- Regulatory delays reinforce concerns about this therapeutic class

Strengths

- Differentiation from Brand X
- Chewable tablets
- Best data
- Perceived to be powerful
- Binds selectively
- Data on its benefit in other diseases

Weaknesses

- No proven economic value
- Perceived to be as much of a pill burden as the competitor products
- Physicians struggle to experience the difference
- Poor targeting
- Its association with 'toxicity' because of the class it belongs to

FIGURE 9.1B   SWOT AFTER THE STRATEGIC REVIEW

What is the deliverable?

For an in-line product a good review of the situational analysis allows you to:

- review/confirm/amend your strategic objectives
- confirm/amend what your marketing effort should be focused on, i.e. the key issues and opportunities that need to be addressed in order to implement the strategy
- confirm (and only very occasionally amend) how you will achieve that focus, i.e. choose those items within your control that will be critical to success
- make decisions regarding next year's non-financial objectives, i.e. what you should now be trying to achieve
- start thinking about implementation, i.e. based on what did and did not work last year, what you might do differently this next year.

What are the challenges?

- **The company process:** For the majority of companies, the requirement for planning 'once a year' is the only occasion used to revisit the situational analysis (or SWOT). Given this, there is a need to consult widely in order to ensure that nothing important is overlooked. For the few companies that rigorously apply monitoring and control processes, the strategic review should be easy, as the lessons learnt will have been incorporated into their thinking on an ongoing basis.
- **What changes to make:** This is not about making changes for changes sake – it is about getting 'under the skin' of the target market, improving understanding and therefore knowledge/insight into why what is happening is happening, and in this way strengthening understanding of the opportunities and threats and how well one is placed competitively (i.e. strengths and weaknesses).
- **The customer vs. the company's perspective:** When undertaking a brand audit, appreciate that when you are sitting at your desk, you are likely to see the world from the company standpoint, whereas your customers (the prescriber, payer, the patient etc.) all have inherently different viewpoints. Successful marketing requires bridging this gap. Remember – you have a brand strategy. With an in-line brand we are not questioning the brand strategy (unless something fundamental to our existing brand strategy has changed). What we are doing is getting to grips with where we are in relation to the brand strategy. Unless you know where you are, how do you know what to focus on in order to implement your brand strategy successfully?

How to approach the review

1. The focus is on the target need-state and all the patient segments embraced by this target need-state.
2. Start with the adjustments that you made to the patient flow. Ask yourself: how has my understanding of the market behaviour improved? Where has it improved? Which segments? Which aspects of the patient flow, and the people influencing this flow, do I now have a better understanding of? Can I use this understanding to improve my explanation

of the opportunities and threats? Refine (edit, amend or delete) the relevant opportunities and threats.

3. Now focus specifically on the prescribing decision. What more have I learnt about how the prescribing decision is made? Have the roles of the various people influencing that prescribing decision changed? What about the decision-makers' attitudes and beliefs about the disease, the different products, about others and about themselves – have *they* changed? Has my understanding or interpretation of these changed? Can I use this understanding to improve my explanation of the opportunities and threats?

4. Now think in terms of the future: what assumptions have we previously made about future events and how these events would impact my target market? Have these assumptions held true? How does what we have learnt this past year help us strengthen and/or amend our interpretation of emerging opportunities and threats?

If you have completed steps 1 to 4 with a small core team, it is advisable to have your thinking challenged by others in the organization. Consider the best forum/events for doing so.

5. Once you have exhausted your review of the external environment (i.e. your opportunities and threats), move on to the internal environment. Here your focus should be on the brand equity that you have.

6. Start with the product audit. Has there been any shift in customer perception as to how well either your brand or competitor brands satisfy the needs? You need to understand why.

7. Focus on those factors that influence or are relevant to building the brand. You need to understand your current brand image. What are the positives? What are the negatives? What programmes contributed to the positives? To the negatives?

   Refer to the latest information that you have on the physicians perceptions of how well the different products satisfy the needs across your target market. This research will help you understand which attributes positively or negatively differentiate one product from another, and which attributes are perceived as being common to the majority of products and therefore not differentiating.

GUIDELINES FOR THE CLASSIFICATION OF OPPORTUNITIES AND THREATS (TABLES 9.1 AND 9.2)

TABLE 9.1   GUIDELINES FOR IDENTIFYING AN OPPORTUNITY

An opportunity is	An opportunity is not
... anything that is outside your direct control and provides a 'way into accessing the market potential'	... something within your control
... something which you and/or your competitors can take advantage of to penetrate the market	... something that is only available to you
... something that exists or may emerge in the near future	... something that you have to create, or do

TABLE 9.2 GUIDELINES FOR IDENTIFYING A THREAT

A threat is	A threat is not
... anything that is outside your direct control and provides a 'barrier to entry' to both you and your competitors	... something within your control
... anything that reduces the potential of the market, i.e. reduces numbers of available patients or reduces the value of the available patients	... something that impacts only you
... something that exists or may emerge in the near future	

8. When updating the brand audit, always keep the two pieces of the puzzle in mind: (a) the customer needs and (b) your brand strategy. Anything that positively differentiates your brand from its competitors is only an asset if it is both relevant to the customer (i.e. satisfies his/her needs) and is aligned to your brand strategy. Likewise, anything that negatively differentiates your brand from its competitors should only be classified as a liability if it is relevant to the customer and is in conflict with your brand strategy. Figure 9.2 illustrates how you might approach this.

9. Those attributes that are relevant to the customer but assumed as being common to all products should be classified as points of parity. Are there any attributes associated with your product which doctors did not mention as being meaningful or relevant to them that could be perceived as positive? List them as potential drivers. Figure 9.2 illustrates how you might approach this.

10. Use this research to update your brand audit and specifically your interpretation of whether strong associations represent a brand strength or weakness.

EXAMPLE

TAKE BRAND X WHERE THE BRAND PROMISE IS AROUND 'DEPENDABLE RELIEF' AND ONE OF THE CORE BRAND VALUES IS 'INTUITIVE'.

LET US IMAGINE THAT THROUGH MARKET RESEARCH WE LEARN THE FOLLOWING: THAT BRAND X IS PERCEIVED AS 'RELIABLE' AND THAT THIS IS A DIFFERENTIATING ATTRIBUTE OF THE BRAND; AND THAT THE SALES FORCE IS PERCEIVED TO BE 'PUSHY AND AGGRESSIVE'.

HOW SHOULD YOU INTERPRET THIS INFORMATION? WELL, THE PERCEPTION AROUND 'RELIABILITY' SHOULD BE INTERPRETED AS A STRENGTH ON WHICH WE CAN BUILD (I.E. WE NEED THE BRAND TO BE PERCEIVED AS DEPENDABLE IF WE ARE TO IMPLEMENT OUR BRAND STRATEGY). WE NEED TO CAPTURE THE VIEW THAT OUR SALES FORCE IS PUSHY AND AGGRESSIVE AS A SIGNIFICANT WEAKNESS (BECAUSE IT PREVENTS THE BRAND FROM ESTABLISHING THE CORE BRAND VALUE OF 'INTUITIVE').

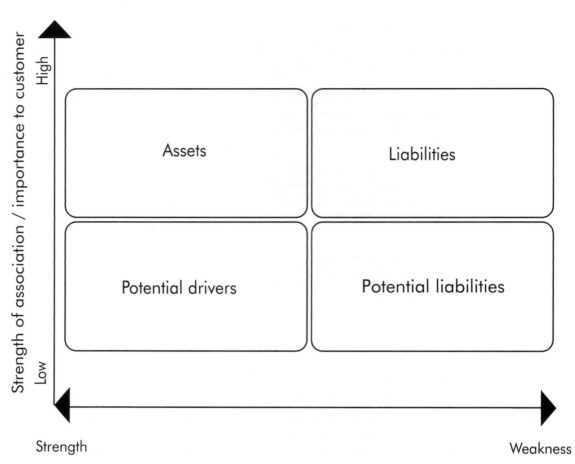

FIGURE 9.2 EXAMPLE BRAND AUDIT

11. Where you have something listed as an asset, describe this as a strength (i.e. something that you have associated with your brand that is working in your favour). Where you have something listed as a liability, describe this as a weakness. Where you have something described as a potential driver, then describe it as a potential strength – it is an association that you either need to make relevant to the customer, or an association that you need to tie to your brand to create competitive differentiation. Where you have something described as a potential liability, then describe this as a potential weakness.

12. Next, focus on the strengths and weaknesses that are not product attributes, i.e. company-related strengths and weaknesses. Has your competitive position changed? Are there items that last year you described as weaknesses that are no longer working against you? Which of the items described as strengths have you been able to hold on to? Which have the competition been able to undermine? Amend the company-related strengths and weaknesses as necessary. However, make sure you are able to explain the amendments you have made (i.e. what has caused this change).

13. Now you should:
    - Review your strategic objectives – are they still reasonable? Are they ambitious enough? Amend as necessary.

GUIDELINES FOR THE CLASSIFICATION OF STRENGTHS AND WEAKNESSES (TABLES 9.3 AND 9.4)

TABLE 9.3 GUIDELINES FOR IDENTIFYING A STRENGTH

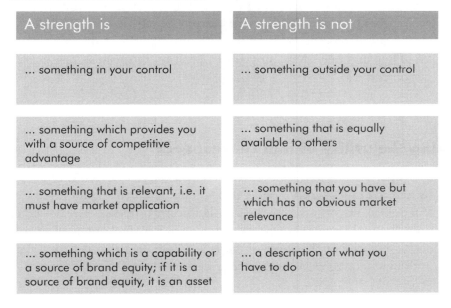

A strength is	A strength is not
... something in your control	... something outside your control
... something which provides you with a source of competitive advantage	... something that is equally available to others
... something that is relevant, i.e. it must have market application	... something that you have but which has no obvious market relevance
... something which is a capability or a source of brand equity; if it is a source of brand equity, it is an asset	... a description of what you have to do

TABLE 9.4 GUIDELINES FOR IDENTIFYING A WEAKNESS

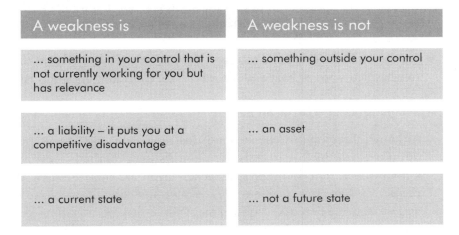

A weakness is	A weakness is not
... something in your control that is not currently working for you but has relevance	... something outside your control
... a liability – it puts you at a competitive disadvantage	... an asset
... a current state	... not a future state

- Revisit the business strategy. This typically describes the target need-state and patient segments that you are focused on and the growth opportunities. It will also talk to the issues that need to be addressed. With regard to the business strategy, aspects such as the growth opportunities, issues and level of investment are occasionally subject to change ... the strategy itself is less likely to be subject to fundamental change. Refine the wording of the strategy *only* if necessary.
- Remind yourself of the brand strategy. The brand strategy describes the core values and the brand essence which best describe the relationship that you want your brand to have with its target market. This is unlikely to change.
- Then refer to the critical success factors. CSFs are those strengths and/or weaknesses that you must invest in to implement the strategy. Confirm the critical success factors. Do the business priorities that were identified last year hold true given the change in

the market situation? One hopes that in the majority of cases, the answer to this question is yes!

The only reason the priorities might change is if the growth opportunities and issues that provided the focus for last year's plan are changed. Even so, the same set of critical success factors may still be relevant. So once again, be wary.

14. Then and only then are you in a position to set next year's goals (i.e. new non-financial objectives).

Maximizing the utility of market research

My experience is that well-structured qualitative research is undoubtedly the best at helping us identify opportunities and threats. This research should be conducted with the decision-maker and any others who have a significant influence on the 'behaviour' you are trying to understand. I know that particularly 'big pharma' feel the need to 'quantify' everything – I am only convinced of the value of doing so if the data that you are quantifying has come from a preliminary qualitative research exercise.

Two points I feel strongly about:

- Insight is the foundation of pharmaceutical brand planning. To develop this, you must go beyond standard research methodologies in order to learn faster and better than your competitors.
- An open mind is critical to interpreting customer insight. Resist the temptation to latch on to what you want to hear and discard other, contradictory information.

When undertaking a brand audit here are some thoughts to bear in mind:

- Although direct approaches towards learning about customers' perceptions can be useful, often it is worthwhile to consider more indirect methods – even some that might appear a bit offbeat. The indirect approaches often are motivated by the assumption that the people we want to research may be either unwilling or unable to reveal feelings, thoughts and attitudes when asked questions. People may be unwilling because they feel such information is embarrassing or private. Alternatively, they may simply be unable to provide the information as to why certain products are prescribed because they don't know the real reason. Projective research techniques address both these problems, in part by allowing the respondent to project themselves into a context, which bypasses the inhibitions or limitations of more direct questioning.
- It really is quite important to use indirect approaches to help you understand what the competitor brands mean to the customer(s). This research should be replicated through time and in the context of different need-states and across the different patient segments. It is inexcusable to be guessing at people's perceptions of the different brands.
- A more direct way to measure associations is to scale the brands upon a set of dimensions. Scaling approaches are more objective and reliable than qualitative approaches. They can be based on a representative sample of customers and uncover the incidence of associations and the relationship among them. In this way they can be quantified.
- Of concern in any one of these studies is identifying the most important perceptual dimensions. One way of obtaining this information is by asking respondents how important each

attribute or benefit is to their choice of brands. The problem here is that often people state everything as being important. A second approach is identifying which attributes discriminate between prescribers and non-prescribers. A third way is asking trade-off questions. The latter technique provides a sensitive measure of dimension importance to a customer. Note that perceptual measurement needs to be done with respect to a specified segment and within the context of a competitive set of brands.

- Another consideration is whether the perceptual dimensions discriminate between brands. If an attribute really discriminates, it might be worth retaining, even though it does not seem important according to other measures (it will be classified as a potential driver). Conversely, if an attribute or benefit patently appears to be important but does not discriminate between brands, then it may be of only marginal usefulness (it will be classified as a point of parity).

Finally, you should not only be interested in the associations with each of the brands, and the position of the brand on the perceptual dimensions, but also in:

- the strength of the association and
- the clarity of the image, i.e. whether customers agree upon the associations with a brand.

Brands with more clarity around their image and with strong associations will prove to be tough competitors.

Frequently asked questions

- **How do I know whether the insight/understanding represents an opportunity or threat?** Refer to the guidelines provided earlier in this chapter for what is an opportunity and what is a threat. Basically, if you feel you need to overcome something, change something about the external environment, or defend yourself from something, it is likely to be a threat.
- **Is correct classification of opportunities and threats important?** In my view it is. Investment in opportunities results in market share gains. Investment in threats might mean market development (which could result in increased sales but maintaining share) or market expansion (again, an increase in sales without necessarily impacting your market share).

  It is especially important that each external factor is recorded as either an opportunity or a threat, rather than as a strength or weakness. Unless it is something you particularly want to invest in, it may not be worth spending too much time debating on which side of the vertical line the external factors end up. That is, do not spend unnecessary energy debating whether it is an opportunity or a threat.
- **Why are we concerned about whether something is a future trend, or already in existence?** It is really very important to develop your understanding of the market as it exists today before you start considering how it might change in the future. This is important because you need to overlay any view about the future onto the reality of today. You cannot consider future changes in isolation. Also, when you do your market forecast, typically you project the underlying historical trend and only then overlay your assumptions about the events that then lead to an adjustment of this underlying trend.

- **Why is it important to focus on your target need-state and patient segments?** When planning for in-line products you are trying to maximize your success. Focus becomes all the more critical. Why spend time and/or money building understanding about parts of the market that you are not interested in? Why not ensure that every dollar spent is spent on improving your understanding of how to implement your strategy or, in exceptional circumstances, amend the strategy itself?
- **Do we need to understand the set of associations from only the physician's perspective or from everyone's perspective?** You do need to understand how your brand is perceived by any customer group you are targeting. If differences exist, then your communication objectives will need to vary. In practice this would mean that the creative idea remains consistent but the associations that you emphasize to different customers might vary.
- **Do we need to determine all strengths and weaknesses from the customer's perspective?** When you are assessing the set of associations linked to your brand and your competitors' brands then, yes, this needs to be done from the customer's perspective. There is no value to the analysis if you do this sitting in your ivory tower making assumptions. However, when it comes to company-related strengths and weaknesses, you will be using competitor intelligence as well.

An activity that you might undertake to help you improve your skill at reviewing the brand situation

1. Get two consecutive copies of a plan for a market/product that you are familiar with. Find the page summarizing the SWOT analysis. Focus on the OT part of the SWOT.
2. Are the opportunities and threats described for the target market only? Are you able to understand the implications from a planning perspective if they are not? Discuss with your colleagues.
3. Focus on the latest copy of the plan. Identify one opportunity and/or one threat that you might refine. How will this refinement affect your implementation plan? What might you do differently as a result of this understanding?
4. Note that if the refinement doesn't lead to you doing something different in practice, you have to question the value of that change.
5. Now compare the latest copy of the plan with the one that preceded it. To what extent had the list of opportunities and threats been refined/strengthened from year to year? Is it immediately apparent how that refinement led to an improved 'tactical plan'? If not, why not? If yes, make sure you can explain why.

Definitions of terms used

- **Assets:** These are attributes unique to the brand and perceived as brand strengths. They build equity. Some assets may be neutralized by competitor activity over time – and therefore would be considered to be 'vulnerable' assets.

- **Attitudes:** How people regard (feel and/or think about) something. Attitudes are more changeable than beliefs.
- **Beliefs:** What people think to be true or not. While beliefs may be more difficult to change than attitudes, beliefs are easier to change than needs, values or motivators.
- **Brand:** The perceptual entity that resides in the mind of the customer and that relates to a product or service.
- **Brand association:** The characteristics of the brand that the customer and/or consumer recall. They can be characteristics that are either liked or disliked.
  This would include thoughts about:
  — the role the brand plays in treatment
  — the differential benefit
  — the brand's emotional relevance to the customer
  — the product attributes/reasons to believe the perceived benefit
  — the brand as a symbol – a visual symbol, or image.
- **Brand audit:** An understanding of the brand's strengths and weaknesses vs. those of the competitors.
- **Insight:** Describes the key reason(s) underpinning the market behaviour they reflect a deep and fundamental understanding of something profound that can be leveraged by the brand to achieve competitive advantage.
- **Liabilities:** These are attributes unique to the brand that detract from the brand equity, brand weaknesses.
- **Market research:** Information used to: identify and define marketing opportunities and challenges; generate and refine marketing actions; monitor marketing performance; and improve the understanding of marketing as a process.
- **Opportunity:** A condition of the environment that makes the realization of potential more likely. Opportunities will include trends that could, potentially, have a positive effect on the market because they will increase or facilitate access to the market. Opportunity is independent of whether or not the company has the capabilities to capture/realize it.
- **Points of parity:** These attributes of the brand are valued by the customer but are not unique to the brand; as a result, they do not differentiate the brand from others.
- **Potential drivers:** These are attributes that are unique to a brand and positive but are not currently valued or associated with the brand by the customer.
- **Potential liabilities:** These are attributes that are unique to a brand and negative but are not currently associated with the brand by the customer.
- **Strength:** Factors within the company/team's control that are required to capture opportunities and/or manage threats. These are both strong and stronger than relevant competitors'.
- **Success factors:** The functions, abilities, power, characteristics of the organization to:
  — capture opportunities and/or
  — manage threats.
- **Threat:** A condition in the environment that is unattractive because it could have a damaging effect on the market. It could be either reducing market potential, or closing the windows of opportunity – regardless of the company's capabilities to manage the condition.

Recommended reading

Aaker, David A. (1991) *Managing Brand Equity*, USA: MacMillan Inc.

Aaker, David A. (1996) *Building Strong Brands*, New York, USA: The Free Press.

Aaker, David A. (2000) *Brand Leadership*, New York, USA: The Free Press.

Blackett, T. and Robins, D. (2001) *Brand Medicine: The role of branding in the Pharmaceutical Industry*, Hampshire: Palgrave Publishers Ltd.

Dogramatzis, Dimitris (2001) *Pharmaceutical Marketing: A practical guide*, Denver, Colorado: IHS Health Group.

Iacobucci, D. (2001) *Kellog on Marketing*, Canada: John Wiley & Sons.

Keller, Kevin L. (1998) *Strategic Brand Management. Building, Measuring, and Managing Brand Equity*, New Jersey, USA: Prentice Hall.

10

Setting New Brand Objectives

In this chapter we will consider:

- What is it that we are trying to do?
- How to set 'new' non-financial objectives
- Maximizing the utility of market research
- Frequently asked questions
- An activity that you might undertake to help you improve your skill at setting non-financial objectives
- Definitions of terms used
- Recommended reading.

What is it that we are trying to do?

With in-line products, many product managers will jump into the fray and start concocting as many marketing programmes as their budget will bear. They perform what I call 'random acts of marketing'; trying this, trying that. They have no clear strategic framework to guide them because they do not really know for sure why consumers buy their product or competing products. In this chapter I am advocating far more structure to the planning approach required for in-line products through the use of non-financial objectives.

The link between the analysis, the understanding that the analysis brings and the eventual actions must be apparent. The situational analysis describes where we are … and the non-financial objectives describe where we need to be by the end of the following year, if we are to succeed in realizing our longer-term strategic objectives. The non-financial objectives are aligned to the strategy. They provide the strategic framework for the tactics. They guide the design of the marketing programme, its development, implementation and evaluation. Appreciate that there is an interdependence between objective setting and budget setting.

While the task of setting objectives can be complex and difficult, it must be done properly because objectives are the foundation on which all programme and budgeting decisions are made. They also provide a standard against which performance can be measured. Meaningful non-financial objectives can also be a useful guide for decision-making. You will often be faced with a number of strategic and tactical programme options. Choices should be made based on how well a particular option satisfies a non-financial objective.

How to set 'new' non-financial objectives

1. Return to your CSFs. For each CSF, decide the role that it is going to play in building your brand. I find the framework proposed by Millward Brown (the 'BrandDynamics™ Pyramid' – see Figure 10.1) a useful one when thinking about the role of the CSF. Let me explain the model and how I use it.

   This BrandDynamics™ Pyramid is used by Millward Brown to measure brand equity. It explains the strength of the relationship that customers have with your brand and allows you to identify which areas of marketing activity it makes most sense for you to focus on.

   I use it to help me with the objective-setting process as follows. I take each CSF and decide which area on the pyramid this CSF will contribute to. I allow myself up to two areas for any one CSF. In this way I make sure that, through my CSFs, I am managing the entire brand building process. As soon as I have decided the role each CSF needs to play in the brand building process, I am in a much better position to set appropriate objectives.

EXAMPLE

IMAGINE THAT I AM RESPONSIBLE FOR THE MARKETING OF ADVAIR (THE ASTHMA MEDICATION). LET'S SAY THAT ONE OF MY CRITICAL SUCCESS FACTORS IS 'EXPERIENCING THE RESULTS WITH ADVAIR'.

IF I LINK THIS TO THE BRANDDYNAMICS™ PYRAMID, I WILL USE THIS CSF TO CREATE 'PERFORMANCE' – I.E. CONVINCE PHYSICIANS THAT ADVAIR ACHIEVES THE RESULTS THEY SET OUT TO ACHIEVE – AND 'BONDING' – CONVINCE THEM THAT NOTHING ELSE BEATS IT. THUS I'VE SELECTED TWO AREAS OF THE PYRAMID WHICH THIS CSF IMPACTS.

SO HOW DOES THIS HELP ME WRITING THE OBJECTIVES?

- WELL, IN RELATION TO PERFORMANCE, WHAT I'M ACTUALLY GOING TO DO IS SET AN OBJECTIVE WITH REGARD TO THE PERCENTAGE OF PHYSICIANS WHO ARE CONVINCED THAT ADVAIR DELIVERS ITS BRAND PROMISE.
- WHEREAS IN RELATION TO BONDING, I WOULD SET MYSELF AN OBJECTIVE FOR THE NUMBER OF PHYSICIANS WILLING TO ACTIVELY PERSUADE THEIR COLLEAGUES TO TRY ADVAIR IN ORDER THAT THEY EXPERIENCE THE RESULTS THAT THEY THEMSELVES HAVE ACHIEVED.

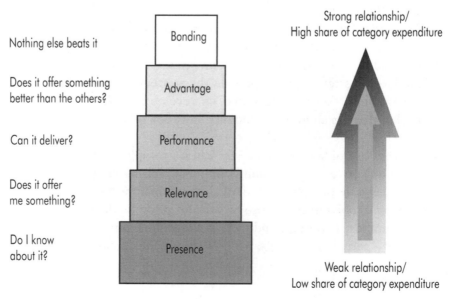

FIGURE 10.1   BRAND DYNAMICS PYRAMID. SOURCE: MILLWARD BROWN'S BRANDDYNAMICS™ PYRAMID

2. I want to ensure that I have at least one CSF addressing each aspect of the BrandDynamics™ Pyramid before starting to write my objectives. Check to ensure that you are managing all aspects of building a brand.

3. Now turn to setting your non-financial objectives. Note that they are statements of outcome. These outcomes are achieved through the implementation of a number of tactics within a given time period. Describe each objective in terms of a specific measurable outcome.

4. Make sure that you retain focus. If you succeed in doing this then at the most you will have two objectives (or outcomes) in relation to a critical success factor, but more often than not, only one. If you are finding it difficult to limit the number of objectives, then you are likely to be describing milestones rather than objectives. Milestones are those interim steps that you must achieve in order to achieve your objective. Do not confuse these milestones with the non-financial objectives.

5. Once you have written objectives in relation to each CSF, ask yourself:
   (a) Are they quantifiable?
   (b) Do they delineate the target market?
   (c) Is there a timeframe for accomplishment?
   (d) Are they realistic and attainable?

If the answer to these questions is yes then the objectives that you have set are likely to be effective (see Table 10.1).

TABLE 10.1 CHARACTERISTICS OF GOOD TACTICAL OBJECTIVES

Characteristics of a good tactical objective	An example of what it might look like	An example of what it is not
An outcome/desired result	X% of physicians believe that Brand X offers dependable control	10% market share
Specific	OR	OR
Measurable	Eight out of ten opinion leaders are actively advocating use of our brand at least on ten occasions a year	Holding four opinion leader workshops before the end of the year
Ambitious		
Realistic		

Maximizing the utility of market research

1. You have to know where you are in order to set appropriate non-financial objectives. This implies the need for tracking your progress from the moment you are active in the market. Below are a list of the aspects that you need to track:
   - Track intuitive brand perceptions against proven prescribing behaviour (cross-analyse one against the other).
   - Track all key brands and analyse referentially/comparatively.
   - Elicit intuitive brand perceptions through the use of enabling techniques, for example:
     (a) scatterboard (key values, terminology)
     (b) coded collages (emotional values)
     (c) bubble diagrams (competitive dynamics).
   - Track messages through carefully constructed batteries of attitudinal statements (reflecting our key messages and those of our competitors).
2. In undertaking tracking research here are some aspects to watch out for:
   - Avoid using generic concepts. Whatever you are testing needs to be comparative, e.g. 'better symptom control than any other agents' etc.
   - Stop asking questions which give you 'nice to know' rather than 'need to know' information.
   - All items on a tracking questionnaire must be 'strategic'.
   - Tighten up the terminology that is being used in the tracking study, e.g. instead of 'lasting efficacy' ask about 12-hour (or 24-hour) control etc.
   - Track both the educational and promotional messages, also emotional and abstract values (personality, beliefs, sensory values and feelings).

Frequently asked questions

- **Is a sales or market share objective a good non-financial objective?** No – one of the most common mistakes that we come across is seeing marketers saying that the objective is simple – to generate sales. To many of you, the only meaningful objective is sales. You will take the position that the basic reason your company invests is to sell its product. It could be your preference to ensure that other members of your team think in terms of how each programme will influence sales, or it could be because you are confusing your strategic objectives with the non-financial objectives. The problem here is twofold. For central marketing groups: if you fail to achieve the desired sales, does this mean that the programmes your team were working on were ineffective? Or does it mean that the pricing strategy did not work? Likewise, for managers in local operating companies: does it mean that the advertising and promotional programme were ineffective? Of course not. The sales results can be due to any of the marketing mix variables and are heavily influenced in our industry by what is happening on the ground (i.e. through the sales force).

  If you are reluctant to write anything other than a sales objective, this indicates that you are uncertain as to what each CSF is expected to contribute to the overall strategy. You are failing to recognize the specific role that the CSF must perform in preparing customers to prescribe a particular medicine, or ensuring that the consumer is committed to taking his/her particular medicine.

- **How many non-financial objectives might be appropriate?** My preference is to maintain the concept of 'focus', which means no more than two non-financial objectives against each critical success factor. This does not preclude you from having a number of milestones below each objective, but it encourages you to have clarity about what precisely it is that you need to achieve.

- **In how many companies do you find the product managers both setting themselves non-financial objectives and measuring progress against them?** Very few. I'm always quite taken aback at how many marketing people in the pharmaceutical industry hate being measured, other than against aspects such as awareness, usage, sales and market share.

  This reinforces my belief that in many cases we do not actually believe that our marketing effort has much impact at all. If sales are not going well then fingers are inevitably pointed at the sales force – what are they doing/not doing?

  Only recently I worked on a project where the client had been running a very visible, high-profile campaign in one country. At the same time, the sales performance for this brand in this country was very good. From a marketing perspective, what was interesting was that the style and tone of the campaign had been extremely consistent over a number of years and this, in the context of good sales, attracted a lot of interest, comment and admiration from others in the same company. What appeared to have passed everyone by was the fact that there was no clear, consistent brand message being communicated. When faced with competition after a few years, the sales performance was difficult to sustain because of the absence of a strong brand message.

An activity that you might undertake to help you improve your skill at setting non-financial objectives

1. Take two different brand plans.
2. Turn to the SWOT analysis in the first brand plan. Keep this in front of you. Now reflect on the strategic objectives for this brand. Then go only to the critical success factors and the corresponding non-financial objectives.
   - In the first instance – link the achievement of the non-financial objective back to the BrandDynamics™ Pyramid. Is the entire pyramid catered for?
   - Next, link the non-financial objective back to the CSF: is each CSF addressed?
   - Finally, consider whether that CSF is a strength or weakness. If a strength: is it clear how far ahead of the competition the brand is? If a weakness: is it clear how far behind the competition the brand is? Now revisit the objectives given where the brand sits within the competitive context: are they appropriate?
3. Where is there room for improvement?
   - Is it in the way the non-financial objective is expressed?
   - Is it in what is trying to be achieved?
4. Compare and contrast your findings with those in a second brand plan.

Definitions of terms used

- **Critical success factors (CSFs):** The critical success factors are the most important conditions that a business must identify and satisfy if it is to be an effective competitor and thrive. They are not objectives in themselves, but they are the factors that play a major role in guiding the company towards business success.
- **Implementation plan:** Specifies the tactics and activities that need to be undertaken to implement the strategy. The implementation plan should clearly define:
  - which non-financial objective(s) will be addressed
  - what tactics are going to be implemented in order to meet the non-financial objectives
  - what action is to be taken
  - priority of action
  - who is responsible for the action
  - how much of which resources (money, headcount, time etc.) will be used
  - when the action is to be started and completed
  - how and when the success/effectiveness of *top* priority actions will be evaluated.
- **Key measures of success:** A component of a marketing plan that reports progress towards achievement.
- **Marketing programme:** Consists of the marketing activities that are undertaken to build brand equity. They cover activities relating to all elements of the 'marketing mix'.
- **Non-financial objectives:** The expression of success regarding critical success factors:
  - Specific
  - Measurable
  - Ambitious
  - Realistic, and
  - Time-limited.

Recommended reading

Keller, Kevin L. (1998) *Strategic Brand Management. Building, Measuring, and Managing Brand Equity*, New Jersey, USA: Prentice Hall.

Kotler, P. (1999) *Kotler on Marketing: How to create, win and dominate markets*, Great Britain: Simon & Schuster.

11

Planning for Implementation

In this chapter we will consider:

- The purpose of a brand plan
- What are the key components of a brand plan?
- How does the need to deliver integrated marketing communications affect the way you approach the design and development of your brand plan?
- Making your communications work
- How to approach the development of the brand plan
- Frequently asked questions
- An activity to help you test your skills
- Recommended reading.

The purpose of a brand plan

Following the review of the external and internal analysis (the situational analysis), you have confirmed your understanding of both the market in which you are going to compete and your current competitive position.

Through your strategic objectives, your brand strategy and your non-financial objectives, you have set out what you are trying to achieve both in the long term and by the end of the following year. Now you need to decide how you are going to make this happen. The brand plan is the document that summarizes the range of tactics that need to be implemented in order to ensure that you are where you need to be at the end of the plan year and on track for achieving your strategic objectives.

What are the key components of a brand plan?

CRITICAL SUCCESS FACTORS

These are the elements (within your control) which define the priorities for future market success. Focusing on them will ensure that you get from your current situation to your strategic objectives and achieve the desired brand position. These critical elements will include two to three critical brand triggers. The critical success factors facilitate the co-ordination of the various groups working to implement the strategy. It is generally agreed that you might have up to five critical success factors (CSFs). No more!

NON-FINANCIAL OBJECTIVES

Non-financial objectives are statements of what is to be accomplished in relation to each CSF, by the overall marketing programme. They are usually defined in terms of specific measurable outcomes. Good non-financial objectives are quantifiable; they delineate the target market and note the timeframe for accomplishment. To be effective, non-financial objectives must be realistic and attainable.

MARKETING PROGRAMME

The primary input to building brand equity comes from marketing activities related to the brand and the day-to-day actions of everyone in contact with the customer. These marketing activities are referred to as the marketing programme and this should be designed in the context of the critical success factors and the associated non-financial objectives. The marketing mix is essentially a conceptual framework, which has been developed to help structure the approach to the marketing programme. There are many different approaches to the marketing mix, e.g. 4Ps, 5Ps and 7Ps etc. They could all be argued to have their limitations, which is why I am keen that we understand the key principle underpinning the marketing mix – that there are a number of building blocks that form the basis of any marketing programme, and that all these variables communicate something about the brand, which is why they need careful consideration.

Below I discuss the 4Ps as a basic and practical framework and explore its application to the pharmaceutical industry. Of particular note should be the great interdependencies among marketing elements. This is what requires the most careful planning. We are now going to discuss these in more detail.

THE FOUR Ps

- **Product strategy:** The product itself is at the heart of brand equity, as it is the primary influence of what the consumers and customers (through patient feedback) experience with a brand. A lot of the communications are also product-centric. For a global marketing team, product strategy is likely to include all activities relating to the clinical development and product development that form the life cycle management plan. For local operating companies, you should consider 'local' clinical trial programmes that might add value to the product experience.

  The delivery system/device/formulation, if it is differentiating, should be used to trumpet some of the 'reasons why'; physicians should prescribe the brand (or believe in the brand promise). It can convey a powerful emotional message which supports your brand promise. The key point here is that many a company falls into the trap of introducing 'new' messages with every new device/delivery system and/or formulation instead of using it to reinforce the most compelling reason to prescribe their brand, i.e. tying it back to their brand strategy.
- **Price strategy:** Think of this as the 'capturing value' activity required to get the product registered, reimbursed and on to local formularies. This typically involves activities around pricing and health economics.

  Remember, everything we do and say communicates something to customers about our brand. This is especially true of our pricing. The price we ask makes a statement about the value we are offering our customers. Physicians do not simply want to prescribe products that are cheap: they are looking for those that offer the highest overall value. If you can convince them that your brand delivers the most value, intrinsically, through the 'reasons why' and by making your brand 'emotionally relevant,' then there will be a willingness to pay a premium for your brand.

- **Place strategy:** The number of countries in which the product is available (its place status) and the manner by which the product becomes available (its reimbursement status) can have a profound impact on the resulting equity and ultimate sales success of a brand. Think of this as the design and management of the regulatory strategy from a global marketing standpoint and the design and management of the access strategy from a local standpoint.
- **Promotion strategy:** Your marketing communications are perhaps the most flexible element of the marketing mix. Marketing communications are the means by which you attempt to inform, persuade and remind your consumers and customers, directly or indirectly, about the brands you sell.

Marketing communications are the 'voice' of the brand and are a means by which it can establish a dialogue and build relationships with consumers and customers. There are wide ranges of vehicles today that you can use to convey your communications (see Figure 11.1).

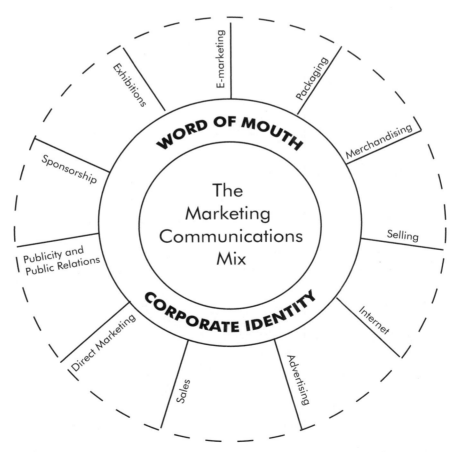

FIGURE 11.1   THE MARKETING COMMUNICATIONS MIX. SOURCE: P.R. SMITH AND J. TAYLOR (2004) *MARKETING COMMUNICATIONS*, 4TH EDN, LONDON: KOGAN PAGE

A MECHANISM FOR MONITORING AND CONTROL

A series of measurements need to be agreed and then actioned to make sure that the plan is implemented. These measurements will cover aspects such as some of the key programmes, through to the attitudes and beliefs and levels of awareness that we need to have in place. This is another important reason for setting specific non-financial objectives, as they provide a benchmark against which the success or failure of the plan can be judged. Without specific objectives, it is extremely difficult to determine what the marketing programme efforts accomplished.

How does the need to deliver integrated marketing communications affect the way you approach the design and development of your brand plan?

The first point is that integrated marketing communications (IMC) requires the recognition of all contact points where the customer may encounter the brand. Each contact point delivers a message – good, bad or indifferent. You should be striving to deliver a consistent and positive message at all contact points.

The second point is that you should be using the multiplicity of contact points available to you – not putting all your money behind one medium. This argues for thinking creatively about which tools you might use.

The third and final point is that not only should your different promotion/education activities be integrated – all four Ps must be integrated. For example, the company cannot intend to charge a high price for its product but provide little in the way of data to support the high price.

Making your communications work

Developing an effective campaign for a brand is not an art, it is the result of strategic discipline, rigorous research and a clear understanding of the relevant and meaningful benefits that make the brand appealing to healthcare professionals and patients. All creative executions need to deliver strong, clear messages that reinforce the 'reasons why' and/or the relevance of the brand, messages that talk to what the brand stands for – the brand essence.

MAKING PR WORK

Public relations is a numbers game. It's a great way to increase exposure to the brand but should always be driven by the *power* of a great idea. Each country needs to develop a PR plan that is innovative and interesting to its own media and package it well.

PR campaigns should develop a momentum that carries them unhesitatingly from the beginning, through the middle and into a well-planned climax. It is a good idea to overlap efforts so that healthcare professionals and patients receive new and slightly different news about the brand from many different media sources. A great PR plan will ensure that each exposure reinforces some aspect of the brand strategy, in a unique and interesting way.

MAKING PROMOTION WORK

Physicians choose to prescribe one product instead of another because they are seeking the benefit that it provides. That's obvious, isn't it?

The challenge one faces is that there is only one point in the whole process where we have a 100% chance to tell the doctor why he should prescribe our brand instead of a competitor brand. This is when he needs to decide what to prescribe. It follows that the best place to trump the competition is exactly at this point: get the benefits of your brand in front of the physician when he is *ready to prescribe*. This is the time when you need to communicate that your product delivers the desired benefit better than any other he might be considering. More often than not, we overlook this apparent 'statement of the obvious'. We mistakenly assume that the physicians know what the product is and what it does, so we just slap the brand name on to a gimmick. That is a big mistake.

MAKING SPONSORSHIP WORK

What should one sponsor? What should one not sponsor?

Sponsorship plays a significant role in the pharmaceutical industry, but how much of the money that we 'give away' in sponsorship is really working for us? Here are some questions that we should ask ourselves before committing to sponsor an event:

- Are a large percentage of our customers interested in this sponsorship event and can one reach them through it?
- Is there a relevant and rational strategic link between this event and the brand strategy? Let us focus on the strategic and creative idea before we commit to the sponsorship.
- Will this sponsorship event provide an effective and cost-competitive media/promotional vehicle?

MAKING EXHIBITIONS WORK

How can we make sure that we always stand out from the crowd?

Every year, thousands of physicians will attend special events such as major congresses, meetings, symposia or conventions. At each event, a large number of pharmaceutical companies will be displaying their wares. How do we ensure that our brand dominates the scene and rises above the throng?

Our brand's pre-eminence at these events will not be coincidental. An effective event plan requires attention to five key areas:

- **Where and how the product is made available for the physician to play with:** While trial data is essential if doctors are to take a new drug into consideration, subsequent loyalties are only built up as prescribers experience the benefits themselves.
- **Attaining a dominant presence through event signage: higher is better:** Keep the design bold, simple and interactive. Avoid fine print and graphical information that would

take too long to digest in such a busy, volatile environment, but do intrigue and challenge your attendees with new insights and interpretations.

- **Effectively linking the event to the brand strategy:** One of the key problems associated with company promotion at big events is that it so often fails to create a relevant connection between the brand and the event. An example of a company that made good use of its advertising dollars is Coca-Cola when its campaign made a clear and logical connection between the brand and the event. The Coca-Cola campaign for the 1996 summer games – 'For the fans' – hit the mark. The underlying strategic premise that Coca-Cola refreshed the fans of the Olympic Games was believable and relevant. The tag line used along with this campaign was 'Cheering is Thirsty Work'.
- **Offering special or preferential treatment to one's guests.**
- **Anticipating competitor activity and planning how to deal with it:** One needs to understand or anticipate the case that might be put forward for our competitors and plan how one wishes to deal with it. You do not want to be caught off guard, you need to understand what the competitors are likely to say and how their messages might be received by your customers.

How to approach the development of the brand plan

Achieving the non-financial objective depends on the proper co-ordination and execution of all the marketing mix elements, including not just promotion but product development, creating the value and access strategies. So before you plan the programmes for the next year, you need to reflect on what you learnt about what worked, did not work and why in the past year. Many of the answers will already appear in the SW part of the SWOT.

This review is important for a number of reasons:

1. **Avoiding costly mistakes:** A lot of money is being thrown about. If a marketing programme is not achieving its objectives, then you need to know about it so that you can stop spending money on it.
2. **Exploring alternatives:** There will always be more than one way 'to skin a cat'. The decision to invest in one programme vs. another is always a tough one. If you have measured the effectiveness of your marketing programmes, then you should be in a stronger position to argue one way or the other.
3. **Increasing the efficiency of your marketing expenditure.**

Described below are my thoughts on how you should go about developing at least the 'bones' of your brand plan.

1. Get a group of people together, including the relevant persons from the following functions: market research, marketing, sales, medical and finance.
2. Everyone should have a copy of last year's CSFs, the corresponding non-financial objectives and this year's non-financial objectives – see the proposed template in Table 11.1. Start with input from market research in terms of what you have achieved in the past year. Using the flip chart, classify the results under two headings: successes and failures.

TABLE 11.1 TEMPLATE FOR REVIEWING LAST YEAR'S MARKETING PLAN

3. Now take the successes and relate these achievements to the CSFs and corresponding non-financial objectives. Reach agreement on which programmes/activities contributed to the success.

4. Look at the next year's non-financial objectives. Where might you apply what worked for you last year, albeit somewhat differently? In this way, you will start building an action plan under each tactical objective.

5. Repeat the process for the elements listed under 'failure'. Relate these to the appropriate CSFs and non-financial objectives. Reach agreement on 'what contributed' to the failure. What might you have done differently? Reach agreement on how you can apply this learning to next year's plan.

6. For each non-financial objective, you will be faced with a number of strategic and tactical options. Your choice should be determined on how well a particular option satisfies the non-financial objective.

7. Before you start planning in detail for each objective, you should describe your overall approach to the marketing programme by thinking specifically around how you are going to ensure that each aspect of the marketing mix is integrated and supports the brand strategy.

8. Next, flesh out in detail the tactics that need to be undertaken. Focus on the objectives one at a time and ask yourself how you are going to go about achieving that objective. List the relevant tactics against each objective. In doing this, do not forget to refer back to what you have learnt from last year.

9. To ensure that you have thought through all aspects of the marketing programme you might find it useful to apply the checklist in Table 11.2.

10. Now cost out the tactics. Are you satisfied that you are spending enough, and doing enough to achieve your tactical objectives? If you're satisfied with the answer to this question, you can now shift your focus to setting up mechanisms for monitoring and controlling progress against implementation of this plan.

TABLE 11.2 CHECKLIST ACROSS COMMUNICATIONS

	Yes/No
Is the marketing mix consistent with required messages?	
Have you got something addressing each stage of the 'building the brand process'?	
Do all activities reinforce the same positioning?	
Is the logo, typeface, pantone colours used in a consistent manner?	
Is the creative approach compatible with image of the brand?	
Does it communicate what it is supposed to?	
Is the creative approach appropriate for the target audience?	
Does the creative approach communicate a clear and convincing message to the customer?	
Does the creative execution keep from overwhelming the message?	
Is the creative approach appropriate for the media environment in which it is likely to be seen?	

Frequently asked questions

- **What guidance can you give me with regard to choosing communication channels?** Always think strategic positioning, think 'Gestalt effect'. Like every other ingredient in the marketing mix, your choice of channel and what you do with that channel must be grounded on sound strategic positioning. This means using the basics of strategic positioning: addressing the **A**udience you are targeting, strongly stating the customer **B**enefit and calling out the **C**ompelling reasons your brand delivers this benefit better than anyone else.

  So, whatever you do, you should always be asking yourself these questions:
  — Which channels are the most relevant to my target customers?
  — How do I communicate the core benefit using each channel?
  — How am I going to reinforce the reasons for my brand (i.e. my key messages)?

- **What questions do I need to ask myself to make sure that each contact is as effective as it could be?**
  (a) Have I done this before? Avoid the temptation to do what you did last year. It is true that, every once in a while, a promotional activity is so compelling, unusual or otherwise remarkable that it will bear repeating, but this is the exception not the rule.
  (b) Is it relevant to my target market?
  (c) Is it implementing our brand strategy?

- **Does the emphasis in the marketing mix vary with the type of brand?** Yes, it is likely to. For example, if you have a functional brand then the pieces of the marketing mix that are likely to enhance performance and/or value for money will be emphasized. This typically means programmes around product, price and distribution take on more importance. If you are creating an image brand then programmes around communication tend to dominate, whereas if you are creating an experiential brand the emphasis is likely to be programmes providing better product experience – typically this means the emphasis is on programmes that facilitate product development, availability and customer service.

An activity to help you test your skills

1. List all the marketing tools that are being used in connection with your brand. Which are the most important? How are you deciding this? Are any tools missing from this list? Why would you say that? Are any tools in the list a waste of money? Can you sort the tools into their roles (i.e. align them to your non-financial objectives)?
2. Are you satisfied with the proportion of funds that you are spending on each promotional tool? Against each objective? If you were going to shift funds, which tools would you reduce and which would you increase? Would you shift the balance of funds allocated to achieving the different objectives?

Recommended reading

Keller, Kevin L. (1998) *Strategic Brand Management. Building, Measuring, and Managing Brand Equity*, New Jersey, USA: Prentice Hall.

Kotler, P. (1999) *Kotler on Marketing: How to create, win and dominate markets*, Great Britain: Simon & Schuster.

Smith, P.R., Berry, C. and Pulford, A. (2000) *Strategic Marketing Communications: new ways to build and integrate communications*, London: Kogan Page.

Smith, P.R. with Taylor, J. (2004) *Marketing Communications* (4th edition), London: Kogan Page.

12

Reviewing the Sales Forecast

In this chapter we will consider:

- What do we need to understand from the sales forecast?
- How to approach the 'strategic' forecast
- How to approach the 'operational' forecast
- Frequently asked questions
- An activity to help you test your skills
- Definitions of terms used
- Recommended reading.

What do we need to understand from the sales forecast?

There are different types of forecasts.

1. There is the sales forecast developed as part and parcel of the strategic planning activities of the business. The business is trying to estimate future revenues and the investment that will be required to generate these future revenues. It uses this information to plan for the future, e.g. does the company need to build more factories? Does the company need to recruit more people?
2. Then there is the sales forecast developed as part of the operational planning cycle. This data is the foundation of the budgeting process, and this influences much, if not all, of the company's activities. Operational planning is highly dependent upon this sales forecast; therefore it is essential to ensure its accuracy.

The importance of the forecast lies in its ability to:

- answer 'what if' scenarios (upside, downside and base case forecasts)
- help define budgets
- provide a basis for monitoring the implementation of the strategy
- aid in production planning.

How to approach the 'strategic' forecast

In Chapter 1 you revisited and revised, as necessary, your market forecast and the 'class share forecast'. In this chapter we are focusing on your future investment and product sales forecast, given your strategy.

At this point, you know:

1. which patients you want to go after
2. the key strategic issues that you are going to focus on and
3. what is going to be critical to success.

You now need to consider how much you need to invest. We start with investment because the extent to which you invest and what you invest in drives the sales.

1. Decide which channels you are going to use to build the brand. Table 12.1 illustrates how you might go about thinking about this.
2. Now refer back to the critical success factors. How are you leveraging your critical success factors? How are they going to be applied to build the brand? Think this through (see Figure 12.1).
3. What, therefore, are the implications for where you invest your money and how you invest?
4. Consider how much you invested last year and in previous years in this channel. With this level of investment were you competitive? Adjust the level of investment to ensure that you are competitive. Remember: if the CSF is a strength then investing as much as the competitors do will ensure that you remain competitive (i.e. ahead). Where the CSF is a weakness you need to invest significantly more than your competitors in order to close the gap (i.e. neutralize this weakness).
5. Once you feel comfortable that you can explain to senior management why you need the funds you do and how you intend to apply those funds, move on to your sales forecast.
6. Start with the market and ask yourself the following question: does our strategy imply market expansion? That is to say, do we intend to invest specifically with the intention of getting more people treated? If yes then, given the level of investment that we are applying, how do we expect to influence the market growth? (Adjust the market growth accordingly.)
7. Does our strategy imply market development, i.e. do we intend that our investment will result in customers using more of the class/category of medication that we are selling? If yes then, given the level of investment that we are applying, to what extent do we expect to influence the share of the class/category? (Adjust class or category share accordingly.)
8. Now move on to considering your patient share of the class/category that you are operating in. Given the level of investment that you are applying this year – compared to last year – how do you expect the pattern of incremental share gain to change? Note that one would assume that if you are investing more than you did last year and that the investment will make you more competitive, then your incremental share should go up, and vice versa.
9. Once you have finalized the forecast for your share of the patient numbers (or patient opportunity), you need to consider how this will translate into sales value.
10. Ask yourself the following question: does our strategy require that the cost per day changes in the foreseeable future? That is to say, does it need to increase or decrease? If yes, then when? Calculate how this will affect the sales value.
11. Does our strategy imply that we will retain patients for longer than we previously have? If yes, then build this into the forecast and adjust the sales value accordingly. Table 12.2 gives you a framework for presenting this forecast.
12. You will need to get both the 'strategic' investment and sales forecast approved before you take next year's sales forecast and work out exactly how much you need to invest each month, and in what, to achieve 'x' level of sales each month. This is known as preparing the budget.

TABLE 12.1   CHANNEL SELECTION

Channel	Presence	Relevance	Performance	Advantage	Bonding
Advertising	✓	✓			✓
Literature			✓	✓	
Patient education					✓
Meetings/symposia	✓	✓	✓	✓	✓
Exhibitions	✓				✓
Professional relations	✓	✓			
Brand reminders	✓				
Market research	✓	✓	✓	✓	✓
Sampling			✓	✓	
Phase IV clinical trials		✓	✓	✓	✓
Sales force		✓	✓	✓	

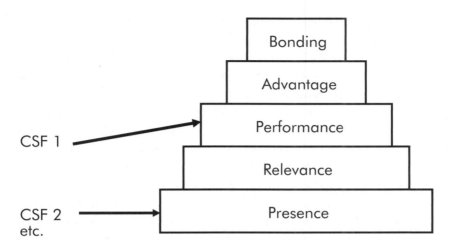

FIGURE 12.1   How do CSFs Apply to Building the Brand?

TABLE 12.2   An Approach to Thinking Through the Forecast

	Current year	Year + 1	Year + 2	Year + 3	Year + 4	Year + 5
Product sales forecast based on underlying trend						
Incremental sales due to investment in market growth						
Incremental sales due to investment in market development (expansion of class/category)						
Incremental sales due to investment in market penetration						
Product sales forecast (total)						

How to approach the 'operational' forecast

1. When you are ready to prepare the budget for the operational plan, my recommendation is that you approach this task as follows:

   (a) Initially work with prescription data not sales value.

   (b) Model what typically happens in the market. On a monthly basis – how many new, switch and repeat patients are there? Does the ratio of new to switch to repeat vary at any time during the year?

2. Now adjust this model in light of your strategy.
   (a) If you are investing in market expansion, when do you expect to see the 'growth' in new patients? Make sure this growth is reflected in an increase in the 'new' patients and over time repeat the patient piece of your model.
   (b) If you are investing in market development, how long will it take before physicians start changing their prescribing behaviour? Make sure this is reflected as an increase in your 'switch' patient and reduction in the 'repeat' patient piece of your model.
3. Now reflect on your competitive position and to what extent your investment is likely to affect your competitive position. Any changes to your competitive position should be reflected in your market share gain of the new and switch patients.
4. Calculate what that means in terms of Rx per month and convert the Rx into value. How close to or far away from your sales forecast are you? This is an iterative process, the key point being that the budget must ensure that the sales team feel that success is constantly within their grasp (so it must be both 'stretching/challenging and realistic' at the same time). What you want to try to avoid is the likelihood that you fall significantly behind budget at the beginning of the year (this can lead to a demotivated sales team – this is not desirable), or that you are too far ahead of budget from the outset (the risk then is that the sales team become complacent with this success).
5. Finally, plan your investment. Think about the pattern of your competitor's investment – how might this influence when you need to invest and how much you need to invest in order to achieve the share gains that you have set out to achieve?
6. What have you learnt about the correlation between the level of, and timing of, this investment and the sales impact? See Figure 12.2. Look at the pattern of the sales forecast and plan your investment in light of this.

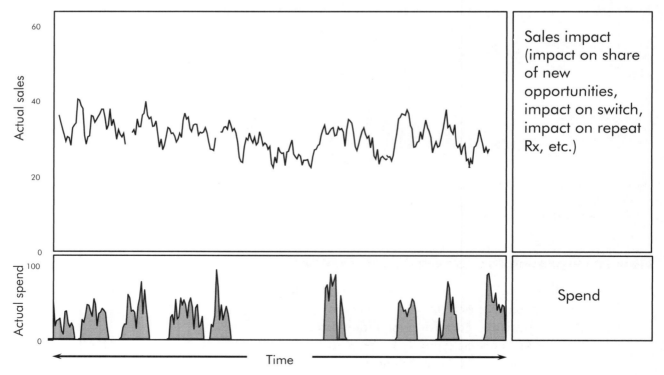

FIGURE 12.2   WHAT IS THE CORRELATION BETWEEN SPEND AND SALES?

Frequently asked questions

- **Surely coming in over budget is better than coming in under budget?** One might think so. The difficulty that I have with both situations is that coming in significantly under or over budget reflects a lack of understanding, either of the market or of the impact of your efforts.

  If we accept the premise that the level of sales we forecast does influence the amount we are given to invest, then if we do better than expected with 'x' level of investment, the question I always ask (but for obvious reasons it cannot be answered) is: how much better could you have done with additional investment? The implication being that you have underinvested in the brand.

- **What is your view about having to cut budgets part way through the year?** This is by no means desirable if you are in the business of building brands. Brand building requires sustained investment over time – how can we ask our customers to trust the brand if for a period of time it is visible and then it is not?

  However, I also accept that the real world is one in which occasionally budget cutting is necessary. The key in this situation is what you cut. Are you being clever about where it is that you are withdrawing funds from, so that you minimize the impact that this reduction in investment has on the customer?

An activity to help you test your skills

Take your sales forecast and see how many people within your team answer these questions in the same way. Note that it is a good idea to get representation from all the disciplines, i.e. sales, marketing, medical, market research, finance, etc.

1. Where are we expecting to get our sales from?
   - How many people answered 'all patients'?
   - How many people answered 'all new patients'?
   - How many people mentioned which product they would displace?
2. How much are we expected to sell this month? This year?

   How much consistency was there in the answers that you got? A lack of consistency suggests that you need to spend more time explaining the strategy and ensuring that people understand the 'numerical implications' of this strategy.

Definitions of terms used

- **Forecast:** The prediction of future events used for planning purposes.
- **Strategic planning:** The process of envisioning a desired future state, defining goals and objectives, and designing marketing and other organizational strategies and tactics to be implemented in the future.
- **Underlying trend forecast:** A standard projection of base data – it uses no other information other than past sales data.

Recommended reading

Dogramatzis, Dimitris (2001) *Pharmaceutical Marketing: A practical guide*, Denver, Colorado: IHS Health Group.

Lidstone, J. and MacLennan, J. (1999) *Marketing Planning for the Pharmaceutical Industry* (2nd edition), Hampshire: Gower Publishing Limited.

13

Building the Brand through Effective Communication

In this chapter we will consider:

- Building brands: the implications
- How to develop integrated communication
- Guidelines for effective communication
- Frequently asked questions
- An activity that you might undertake to help you improve your skill at reviewing the size of the market
- Definitions of terms used
- Recommended reading.

Building brands: the implications

The brand implies a promise to customers and a commitment by the organization. Brand building is therefore more than a communication and packaging programme. It needs an investment programme with a timetable and budget.

Given that prescribing patterns and perceptions of a product may vary from one country to another, so will the purpose of the brand communication. For example, the task of sharpening a diffused image is quite different from the task of changing a very tightly established one. This means that the communication approach must be adjusted to address the different problems that you might face in different markets.

Marketing and/or communication activities will typically be directed towards one of two outcomes: either reinforcing the current positioning in order to sustain it over time, when this is already aligned with the brand position strategy or, alternatively, shifting positioning perceptions to match the target market's needs more closely and match the desired brand position strategy.

The purpose of this chapter is to consider current best practice in the development of integrated communication.

How to develop integrated communication

1. Develop an understanding of why you are where you are. This is known as the communication process analysis.

   To do this analysis, you need to gather as much current information as possible about your brand as well as the brand status of key competitors. Specifically you are interested in assessing:
   - your own and competitive communications
   - key messages (copy)
   - visuals (art direction)
   - elements (logo, colours, tag lines, etc).

   Remember, you are doing this analysis to try to understand why you are where you are. Is it because the competitors have a more effective brand position then you do? Is it because their communication is more or less consistent? Is it because their communication is more or less clear? Which aspects of their communication have threatened/could potentially threaten your brand strategy? Therefore, what implications might this have for the way in which you communicate?

2. Gather customer insight – to communicate effectively requires customer insight. Two types of insight are important. One relates to what the customer believes about the brand and the category in which it holds membership. The other type of insight is regarding how the customer uses this information to make brand decisions. This insight is the basis for planning all communications and is best undertaken on a country-by-country basis.

3. Commission the appropriate research. Customer insight emerges from conducting in-depth interviews, focus groups and surveys. Knowing what customers think must provide a starting point for all communication. Equally important is 'how' customers think and, more specifically, how they process and use information.

4. Brief the agency – ultimately, as a result of this analysis you need to:
   - state the current belief that you want to feed or change
   - state the desired future belief
   - produce a clear statement of the purpose of your communication
   - write a statement that communicates the brand message
   - summarize what you have learnt about customer beliefs regarding the brand and the category in which it holds membership, and how they process and use information.

   When briefing the agency to develop the creative idea, try to conform to an accepted belief. Only when this is not possible because the brand's equity is not consistent with accepted consumer beliefs should the knowledge of the customer's beliefs serve as a basis for developing counter-arguments to change their disposition.

   Also, note that differentiation is absolutely critical for smaller players, whereas strength of association is important for brands which are dominant.

5. Secure the creative idea – at the heart of brand building is the customer insight that underpins the development of the brand strategy. The creative idea is the central concept around which a set of co-ordinated programmes can be developed. A good creative idea guides the execution of the brand strategy, and will precipitate programmes that:
   - build the brand by creating visibility, associations and relationships that are relevant to the customer
   - break out of the clutter.

   The creative idea is inspired by customer insight. It can emphasize any aspect of the brand. For example, Figure 13.1 demonstrates an execution which emphasizes the emotional relevance of the brand Zofran™, whereas Figure 13.2 demonstrates an execution which emphasizes the functional benefits of the E45 brand and Figure 13.3 demonstrates an execution emphasizing what the Losec brand stands for (i.e. its attitude).

FIGURE **13.1**   EXAMPLE OF BRAND COMMUNICATION EMPHAIZING EMOTIONAL BENEFITS. CAMPAIGN LAUNCHED IN 1990. COMPANY: GLAXO. AGENCY: PALING WALTERS

FIGURE **13.2**   EXAMPLE OF BRAND COMMUNICATION EMPHASIZING FUNCTIONAL BENEFITS. COMPANY: CROOKES HEALTHCARE. AGENCY: TORRE LAZUR MCCANN HEALTHCARE LONDON

FIGURE 13.3   EXAMPLE OF BRAND COMMUNICATION EMPHASIZING WHAT THE BRAND STANDS FOR.
COMPANY: ASTRAZENECA. AGENCY: LANE, EARL AND COX

6. Evaluate the creative idea through asking yourself the following questions:
   - Does it resonate with customers?
   - What brand building programmes could surround it?
   - What associations could and would be developed?
   - How visible would it make the brand (consider ability to enhance recognition, facilitate recall, and make it 'top of mind')? In other words, will it break out of the clutter?
7. Test several executions of the creative idea before committing to any one execution – see Table 13.1 which provides a checklist for a discussion guide designed to test the effectiveness of communication.

TABLE 13.1   CHECKLIST

A checklist for a discussion guide designed to test effectiveness of communication
Are the objectives of the research explained?
Has provision been made to elicit what the respondents already know, understand, believe and/or feel about our brand before they are exposed to new/different communication?
Is there provision for spontaneous recall before the structured assessment of the communication is undertaken?
Is the respondent asked to prioritize, e.g. main message? Or most compelling message?
Are the questions being asked likely to elicit both rational and emotional insight?
Do you understand the analytical framework that the agency is going to use to interpret the research results?

8. When testing:
  - Test the finished execution of the creative idea using a minimum of six ads.
  - Test the finished execution always in the same position – usually the second position. This ensures that there is a context for looking at it. The other ads needs to be rotated.
  - Judge the creative idea, not the execution.

Guidelines for effective communication

The common mistakes that consistently damage campaigns in the pharmaceutical industry include:

  - **Putting your logo everywhere:** Never produce a communication that states only the company or brand name. Always have a relevant message linked to the brand or company name that reinforces your brand strategy.
  - **Indulging yourself on fabulous and expensive images that do not bother to connect the customer with the brand:** Never use imagery in your advertising that does not *relevantly link and support* your brand image or personality or its usage occasion to the conceptual target. Always develop advertising in which the customer (conceptual target) can 'insert' him or herself into the picture. If you succeed in getting the customer to visualize themselves in your advertising, the battle is won.
  - **Imitating a competitor's campaign instead of carving out one's own unique identity:** Never produce advertising that looks anything like something that your competitor is currently running or has run in the past. Always ensure that your campaign is different, better and special, convincing customers of the unique nature of your brand and communicating the benefits of purchasing your products.
  - **Making a claim that you cannot support:** Never oversell your product benefits by stretching the truth. Never develop advertising that puts your brand in a position that customers find hard to believe. Always communicate clear, meaningful benefits, backed up with rational and believable 'reasons why'.
  - **Trying to be trendy by borrowing from today's news or culture:** Never jump on a trend as the genesis for your advertising creative.
  - **Advertising that attacks or is angry in tone:** Few people tolerate abrasive communication through more than a few repetitions. Never use anger – it turns people off.

Frequently asked questions

  - **What are the most common mistakes that people make in developing campaigns?** There are two common mistakes:
    (a) When you review campaigns from dozens of different companies in the market in which you compete, you will be shocked to see that many of the executions appear almost identical and could be interchanged without anyone noticing which company they are from.
    (b) The other common mistake is that the communication fails to create a relevant connection between the brand and the target market.

- **Can we communicate several messages at once?** No, you should only ever have one brand message that supports the brand position. This brand message may be communicated using different vehicles and each vehicle may reflect different components of the brand message. But there is only ever one brand message. The brand message changes over time.

  The most important thing, in times of both war and peace, is to provide a single, consistent voice to the outside world. Make sure that everything the press, your customers and your consumers hear and see about your company and brand is accurate and conforms to the corporate image and individual brand positioning strategy.

- **With an in-line brand, who is our first obligation to? New or existing customers?** The first obligation with an existing brand is to your current customers, and especially to your heavy prescribers. When a brand is in erosion, the obligation is to halt the decline, which typically involves focusing on current users. When other customer segments are considered for targeting, it is critical to assess the impact on current users. The brand's equity lies with existing prescribers and/or users. This is not to say that you should never abandon the brand's equity. However, there needs to be a compelling reason to do so.

- **Do any campaigns stick out in your mind as brilliant executions, offering a clear understanding of why that particular brand should resonate with the customer?** Yes – Figure 13.4 to 13.6 illustrate the campaigns that in my view were groundbreaking when they were introduced.

- **Does the emphasis in the marketing mix vary with the type of brand?** Yes, it is likely to. For example, if you have a functional brand then the pieces of the marketing mix that are likely to enhance performance and/or value for money will be emphasized. This typically means programmes around product, price and distribution take on more importance. If you are creating an image brand, then programmes around communication tend to dominate, whereas if you are creating an experiential brand, the emphasis is likely to be programmes providing better product experience – typically this means the emphasis is on programmes that facilitate product development, availability and customer service.

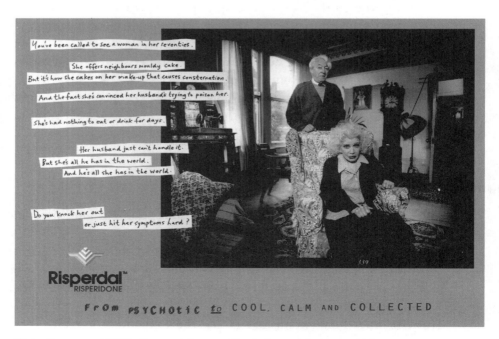

FIGURE 13.4   RISPERDAL (1997). COMPANY: JANSSEN-CILAG. AGENCY: JUNCTION 11 ADVERTISING

FIGURE 13.5   SERETIDE (2002). COMPANY: GLAXOSMITHKLINE. AGENCY: TORRE LAZUR MCCANN HEALTHCARE LONDON

FIGURE 13.6   ZESTRIL (1997). COMPANY: ASTRAZENECA. AGENCY: MCCANN HEALTHCARE

- **Who should be in charge of branding?** Nobody is in charge as such – everyone has a role to play!

  Senior management must demonstrate that internal brand alignment is a high priority for everyone in the company through their own commitment to the achievement of brand goals, brand values and behaviours. Through words, and the actions and the initiatives they support, senior managers can demonstrate that the whole company is serious about branding. Functional barriers must be broken down. The focus of everyone's day-to-day activity must be to deliver superior performance on the brand triggers. It is all about strong, and distinctive, delivery against the critical success factors.

Middle managers are the key to delivering the brand promise. Their role is to infuse their teams and their operations with a practical commitment to living the brand. This applies as much to 'back office' functions, such as sales support, as to sales and medical information.

Marketers play a critical role in identifying the brand triggers that can be the pathway to stronger brand equity and ensure the creation of appropriate communications and programmes to reinforce and personalize the messages.

- **Who should be in charge of the brand?** The challenge of developing a global brand is usually inhibited by local brand teams. The limitation of this is the belief that their market situation is unique and that customer insights and best practices from other markets do not apply to them. The local brand team may also feel, perhaps subconsciously, that its freedom to act is being inhibited and that it is being coerced or enticed into a sub-optimal strategy.

  To deal with this challenge, someone or some group needs to manage the global brand. If there is no motivated person or group accountable for the global brand synergy – it will not happen.

  Some ideas include:
  - **Brand champions:** The brand champion needs to have both credibility and respect and so by definition must be a senior executive. He/she might sit in one of the local operating companies. A brand champion would, for example, approve all brand stretch decisions. He or she must identify insights and best practices and propagate them by suggestion.
  - **Business management teams:** The idea here is essentially that each therapeutic area is run by a team consisting of managers with line responsibility for R&D, manufacturing, and marketing and sales etc. The team is chaired by an executive vice-president with a second-line job – for example, a general manager. The business management team define the brand character and position for all brands in that therapeutic area. They manage the creation of local brand building excellence that can become a global success model. They also manage product innovation.
  - **A global brand manager:** Here an individual is charged with creating a global brand strategy that leads to strong brands and global synergy. Their primary role is building and protecting brand equity. The global manager develops, adapts and manages the internal brand communication system. In fact, not just manages it, but becomes a key part of it. By learning about customers, problems and best practices throughout the world, he or she is in the best position to define and communicate opportunities for synergy.
  - **Global brand teams:** This is probably the most common model employed in the pharmaceutical industry. Typically the global brand team will consist of brand representatives from different parts of the world. The job of the global brand team is to manage the brand globally. The keys to success are an effective global brand planning process, a global brand communication system, the right people on the team and support from top management.

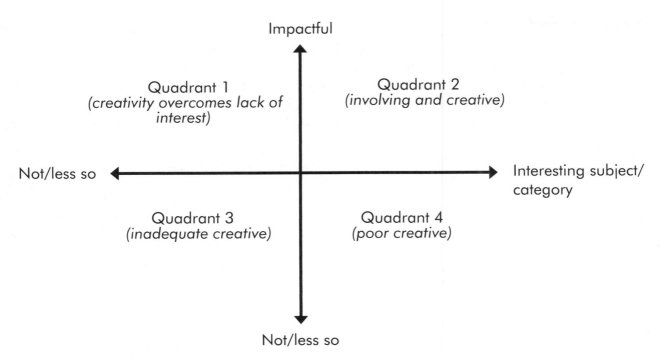

FIGURE 13.7 ASSESSING IMPACT OF COMMUNICATION

An activity that you might undertake to help you improve your skill at reviewing the size of the market

An important consideration is whether the execution of the creative idea is sufficiently impactful. Take a range of pharmaceutical ads – include your own.

Decide where they fall given the matrix in Figure 13.7. Of all the ads that you look at, what proportion falls into quadrant 2? (Not many, I bet.) How many that need to fall into quadrant 1 actually end up in quadrant 3? (Quite a few is my presumption.)

This activity hopefully goes some way to highlight one of the opportunities in effective communication – being seen!

Definitions of terms used

- **Communications process analysis:** Gathering, analysing and interpreting information on what customers think.
- **Customer insight:** Describes the key reason(s) underpinning the market behaviour.

Recommended reading

Keller, Kevin L. (1998) *Strategic Brand Management. Building, Measuring, and Managing Brand Equity*, New Jersey, USA: Prentice Hall.

Smith, P.R., Berry, C. and Pulford, A. (2000) *Strategic Marketing Communications: new ways to build and integrate communications*, London: Kogan Page.

Smith, P.R. with Taylor, J. (2004) *Marketing Communications* (4th edition), London: Kogan Page.

14

Monitoring and Controlling the Implementation of the Brand Plan

In this chapter we will consider:

- What is meant by monitoring and control, and why is it necessary?
- What are the key considerations in developing your approach to monitoring and control?
- Frequently asked questions
- An activity to help you test your skills
- Recommended reading.

What is meant by monitoring and control, and why is it necessary?

You will know that you need to assess the implementation of your strategy so that you can innovate, learn from past failures as well as successes, and identify knowledge gaps. My question is: how many of you do monitor much more than sales?

Even more revealing are the answers to the question, 'What do you need to monitor?' In many cases the answer to this question is a list of data sources or types of research rather than a clear understanding of what factors need to be monitored. So, although everyone agrees that research is required, there is little agreement on what needs to be monitored.

For what it is worth, I will share with you what I believe companies should be monitoring and why they should be monitoring these aspects.

- **Performance ($) (absolute, growth and market share):** This informs senior management as to whether we are achieving the goals that we set out to achieve.
- **Behaviour (Rx for which need-state and patient segment):** This informs us whether we are getting our sales from our target need-state and the associated patient segments or from our target customer segment(s). An indicator of effective implementation of the brand strategy.
- **Achievement against non-financial objectives:** This informs us whether the investment that we are making is effective.
- **Key messages:** What factors/claims are associated with the brand; has a 'reason why' been established? This informs us whether we are effectively building the desired brand position and brand character.
- **Brand health:** Status and stature; the extent to which the product is rationally and/or emotionally prescribed; how it resonates, i.e. tone and style. How the brand is doing against its competitors – this informs us as to whether our strategy is working, whether it needs to change. Finally, what can we learn about our competitors to use to our advantage?

- **Marketing effectiveness:** Is what we are doing effective? What are we saying that is effective? This informs us about whether our programmes are effective and, if so, which ones. Also about whether our communicationa are effective and, if so, which communications.
- **Competition:** What is it showing that could be problematic? This helps us predict future vulnerabilities.

What are the key considerations in developing your approach to monitoring and control?

QUESTIONNAIRE/STUDY DESIGN

The agreed convention is illustrated in Figure 14.1.

ANALYSIS

Several points here:

1. Ideally, you need to ensure that we understand which people have seen the advertisement or the promotional material and which have not. Only then can we attribute the communication to the difference in result.
2. The analysis process is key – for example, a bigger brand will get more mentions than a smaller one – so everything needs to be interpreted relative to the brand's size before identifying distinguishing features.

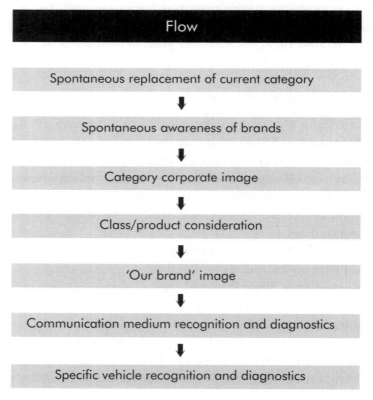

FIGURE 14.1   QUESTIONNAIRE DESIGN

3. Understanding the agencies' analytical framework is important – the analysis and interpretation of the research is as important as asking good questions in the first instance.

TIMING

You need to know what your customers have been exposed to in terms of both your own and competitor communication in order to understand the results of the research. Typically, you want to measure 'pre' and 'post' exposure to the specific communication.

THE BRAND MUST BENEFIT

If we agree that in monitoring and controlling the implementation of your brand strategy one of the significant benefits is the learning that is associated with this process, then surely an equally important consideration is ensuring that you have a framework or process for managing this knowledge. Which of the following knowledge management strategies are you applying? Could you benefit from others?

- **Leveraging the knowledge that exists:** Here the focus is on transferring what you have learnt throughout the organization and/or making sure that you are learning from others within your organization. In many companies we work with, this is formally implemented through their 'sharing best practice' schemes.
- **Expanding your knowledge:** Have you identified those areas in which you are barely touching the surface? Where is there considerable potential for new learning? Bring in additional expertise. Today in the pharmaceutical industry there is evidence of bringing in people with 'packaged goods' backgrounds, economics etc.
- **Appropriating knowledge:** This strategy is about transferring knowledge from external sources, gaining strategic insight through everyday life. A number of the activities described in this text are about appropriating knowledge. Try it – you may be surprised by what you learn.

Frequently asked questions

- **Give us one tip in relation to monitoring and control:** The 'brand strategy' needs to be well defined – otherwise what are you measuring?
- **Given limited resources, what should you spend your research monies on?** On improving our understanding of the market or on monitoring implementation of our strategy? Appropriate monitoring must take priority. You need to be sure that your strategy is being implemented effectively. However, the moment you identify an issue with regard to implementation, you will need to go back to the market and challenge the insight that underpins your strategy and the execution of the strategy.
- **Are you an advocate of testing the detail aid once it is in the field?** No, I am not. If you tested it before going to print and refined it in line with the findings and conclusions from that piece of research, what are you going to do with the findings, given that you have now printed large quantities and distributed them to your representatives? With a new campaign my belief is that what you should really be trying to understand is the following:
  — What are the immediate effects?
  — Have the communications contributed?
  — Which ones and how much?

You can learn from this and apply that learning to the next campaign.

- **How do you know whether you have a strong brand?** You will not be able to answer this question by looking at your market share. Nor by looking at your sales value or performance against budget. Only by measuring brand equity. Market research companies such as Millward Brown have developed tools to measure 'brand equity'.

For any marketer faced with writing a brand plan, a starting point has to be establishing the current strength of your brand or service; that is, understanding your brand equity.

Within the pharmaceutical industry, there are very few companies that can answer the question I posed. Only three companies that we work with are measuring brand equity as a matter of routine, although there are indications that some of the leading companies are trying to set up a research process to gather the necessary information. The big question is whether, when budgets come under pressure, measuring brand equity survives even in these large companies. The only reason it will, is if senior management believe in branding.

An activity to help you test your skills

Find an example of two recent (but different) campaigns for the brand you are working on. See whether you can answer the following questions:

- Which one 'pulls the customer in' better and why?
- How do physicians read the ad?
- What did physicians remember about each ad – and why?
- Which campaign involved the brand better – and why?

If you struggle to answer these questions then you are not doing enough in terms of monitoring and control and capturing the learnings.

Recommended reading

Iacobucci, D. (2001) *Kellog on Marketing*, Canada: John Wiley & Sons.
Keller, Kevin L. (1998) *Strategic Brand Management. Building, Measuring, and Managing Brand Equity*, New Jersey, USA: Prentice Hall.
Levy, Sidney J. (1999) *Brands, Consumers, Symbols & Research*, California, USA: Sage Publications, Inc.

Conclusion

Overcome the challenges

There are special challenges for branding in the pharmaceutical sector. These include:

- **The time you have to develop and milk the brand:** This is short because of the short patent life and widespread usage of generics post patent expiry.
- **The approach to building the brand:** Physicians value science-based brand choices. This needs to be recognized in the way communications are approached. Choosing a 'poor' brand will undermine the physician's relationship with the patient and can have legal ramifications. Regulatory constraints are prominent and affect new product development and brand promotions.
- **Managing consistency in communications across multiple audiences:** Government and insurance schemes mediate brand choices through formularies and reimbursement criteria, so we must also have messages that are meaningful to them.

Adopt a customer focus – it is an essential ingredient

The marketing function within the pharmaceutical industry needs to change rapidly. It has to become more customer-focused in order to be able to build brands.

While not the only measure of success, it is generally recognized that companies which understand how to maximize the value of the customer base have greater long-term value than companies which are simply product-focused. This is not to say that the products and services offered by the company are not important, but that true long-term value is being driven more and more through the customer base.

In my view, brand planning helps to maximize the long-term value of the customer through three different mechanisms:

(a) customer acquisition – getting the medication used in the 'right' situation (i.e. the right physician and patient)
(b) customer loyalty – getting the 'target' physicians to prescribe our brand more of the time
(c) customer retention – patients staying on medication for longer.

Don't avoid segmenting and targeting

Segmenting and targeting are two of the primary marketing concepts underpinning brand planning. Their purpose is to reduce the universe of potential customers (be it physicians or patients) to a smaller number but those that remain are much more likely to respond to the company's offering. Thus segmenting and targeting are critical elements of efficient and effective brand planning.

The thoughts, memories and feelings that people have about a brand are, at an individual level, the essence of brand equity. Creating and maintaining that equity requires creating value in the 'factory' and in the minds of the customers (physicians, payers, patients, other healthcare providers etc.). The challenge with managing an in-line brand is maintaining and strengthening the equity.

Clarify the roles and responsibilities of the central team vs. the local markets

MY RECOMMENDATION WITH NEW PRODUCTS

As discussed previously, there are a number of major decision points involved in the 'Brand Planning for New Products' scenario, namely: the market segmentation approach (need-states and patient segments); the strategic objective; targeting (need-state, patient segments and customers); the brand strategy; the critical success factors; and actions. Who should be taking these decisions? Should they be taken at the centre, or by regional marketing teams, or by the local marketing teams?

I am a great believer in 'think global, act local'. Regional marketing teams, in my view, can add a lot of value in facilitating the implementation of the 'think global' piece while ensuring that the implementation plan addresses all the local issues.

In support of this approach, there is a need for a global marketing function and a local operating company marketing function. The regional marketing function is probably a 'luxury' for those with a global marketing function, but a necessity for those without. Our experience suggests that there are six sub-processes which are primarily driven by a central marketing function; they are:

- strategy and planning
- researching the market
- preparing the market
- preparing the company
- capturing product value (regulatory and reimbursement strategies)
- life cycle management.

The other processes ('developing the product', 'obtaining approval' and 'making the product available') are primarily the responsibility of R&D and manufacturing functions.

The local operating company involvement will vary depending on the lead time to launch. It should be very involved in researching the local market, preparing the local market and the 'access' strategy pre-launch.

In an ideal world, the local marketing team involvement really starts in earnest about two years prior to launch, although commercial input (co-ordinated centrally but endorsed locally) is necessary from the proof of concept stage when the strategy and development plan is being formulated.

In Tables A (1), A (2) and A (3) you will find a summary of my perspective on the respective contributions of the local operating company and a central marketing team in the run up to launch. Will examine three stages: 24–36 months pre-launch; 12–18 months pre-launch; and launch!

TABLE A (1)   THE RESPONSIBILITIES OF CENTRAL VS. LOCAL MARKETING TEAM (24–36 MONTHS PRE-LAUNCH)

24–36 months pre-launch
Centrally produced strategic plan
This will be a centrally produced plan based on the clinical data available and likely target product profile, competitive position and market environment
The local operating companies review the plan (preferably in face-to-face meetings). The intention is that the global marketing team consolidates the input to develop the brand strategy
Researching the market
This requires local operating company participation and co-funding of the early market research to confirm the market environment, competitor position and attitude to target product profile. Research should include physicians, patients (depending on the disease state) and the payers
Preparing the market
The global marketing team will be seeking local recommendation on thought leaders for the global pre-launch preparations

TABLE A (2)   THE RESPONSIBILITIES OF CENTRAL VS. LOCAL MARKETING TEAM (12–18 MONTHS PRE-LAUNCH)

12–18 months pre-launch
The key milestone at this time is the availability of phase III clinical data so the actual product profile is known
Centrally produced strategic plan
The global marketing team updates the plan with clinical data and the product profile and incorporates local input from previous review to refine the proposed brand strategy
The local operating companies are asked to review the updated plan
The local operating companies are asked to prepare their launch plan
Researching the market
The local operating companies are asked to participate and co-fund central market research to finalize the brand strategy
The local operating companies are asked to prepare their market research to support launch
Preparing the market
Local operating companies initiate local advisory boards, utilizing their members from the global panel
Local operating companies provide the audience for centrally sponsored symposia, educational activities and the global 'launch' meeting
Local operating companies liaise with their respective health authorities to get the product reimbursed and/or available on formularies (as necessary)
Preparing the company
The local operating companies attend the central 'train the trainers' meetings
The local operating companies customize the central training materials for local use
Local operating companies develop and test local promotional materials
Local operating companies prepare the local companies for launch
Capturing product value
The local operating companies utilize the centrally developed pricing and health economic data to obtain best local price /reimbursement within corporate defined price band

TABLE A (3)   THE RESPONSIBILITIES OF CENTRAL VS. LOCAL MARKETING TEAM (LAUNCH)

Launch
The local operating companies launch the product and provide feedback on success/issues/performance to central team on both a formal and informal basis
The global marketing team shift their emphasis to creating the value strategies and the product life cycle plan which supports the brand strategy

MY RECOMMENDATION WITH IN-LINE BRANDS

For an in-line brand, the role of a central team is to support the implementation of the global brand strategy through the life cycle plan. The central team's efforts should be focused on decision-making around aspects such as:

- Which indications to continue to support and strengthen the brand position?
- Which data is required in ongoing support of the key messages?
- What product developments/formulation developments might be required to keep the brand relevant and/or to support the brand position?

The local marketing teams, on the other hand, should be concerned with the effectiveness with which they are communicating where the brand has relevance, why it has relevance etc.

Regional marketing teams, in my view, can add a lot of value in facilitating the implementation of the 'think global' piece, while ensuring that the implementation plan addresses local issues.

In support of this approach, there is a need for the marketing research money now to be spent by the operating companies to ensure they understand their customers, what they have achieved (or not) with their customers, and why they have achieved what they have achieved.

In Table B (1) you will find a summary of my perspective on the respective contributions of the local operating company and a central marketing team in the management of an in-line brand.

Get the whole organization to support the brand

Your marketing team must articulate a distinctive and relevant brand positioning and identify the two or three critical triggers supporting the brand promise that will establish the foundation for building an emotional bond with the customer. These should be identified as critical success factors in your marketing plan.

The brand strategy identifies the desired associations, which in turn will drive all aspects of the marketing effort. Any form of customer contact should consider how it can create or strengthen the desired associations.

TABLE B (1)   A FRAMEWORK FOR 'THINKING GLOBALLY, ACTING LOCALLY'

| Market segmentation |
| This will be centrally developed with local market input |
| Strategic analysis |
| Both the global brand team and local markets should be required to do this. The output from this is identification of strategic issues/opportunities |
| Brand strategy |
| Defined centrally, monitored and controlled locally |
| Brand building programmes |
| Global teams to action brand building through life cycle management |
| Markets to identify breakthrough brand building programmes locally and then share through best practice forums |
| Goals and measures |
| Strategic goals and measures should be defined |
| Short-term goals and measures defined by the markets |

The critical success factors will vary depending on whether we are looking at the global marketing plan or a local operating company plan. Even if it is a local operating company plan, there may still be variance between the critical success factors of each local operating company.

My recommendation is that each of the support functions takes the set of critical success factors and writes their own objectives against these critical success factors. These objectives need to be aligned to the strategic objectives and the brand strategy. In this way you can be assured that all the functions are aligned to the marketing plan, whether they are global functions or local operating functions.

Finally, your senior team as a whole must mobilize the organization to act on the critical success factors. You must integrate the consistent execution of these core brand delivery triggers into the operations. To do this, they need to constantly check to ensure that the critical success factors are incorporated into the normal stream of organization activity (for example, day-to-day roles, specific processes such as business planning, operational metrics) rather than being items that are actioned by only the marketing department.

Create a structure

Strive to achieve: well-defined vocabulary; the same strategic analysis inputs; the same structure; and the same outputs.

The bulk of the text in this book addresses the first three points – I am now going to share with you my thinking on output.

AN OUTLINE STRUCTURE FOR THE NEW PRODUCT 'BRAND PLAN'

The new product plan is best presented as a Word document. This allows you to communicate a lot of the learning which underpins the thinking around positioning, etc. I am including an example table of contents for the new product strategic brand plan. Different sections might require emphasis depending on how early in the clinical development process the product you are managing is.

EXAMPLE

1. PRODUCT PROFILE
2. MARKET SITUATION
    a PREVALENCE AND INCIDENCE
    b MARKET PLACE
    c MARKET ECONOMICS
    d UNMET NEED
    e COMPETITIVE DIFFERENTIATION
    f SWOT ANALYSIS
3. KEY ISSUES
4. STRATEGIC OBJECTIVES
5. THE BRAND STRATEGY
6. CSFs AND TACTICAL OBJECTIVES
7. THE MARKETING PROGRAMMES
8. KEY MEASURES OF SUCCESS
9. APPENDIX
    APPENDIX 1: PATIENT FLOW
    APPENDIX 2: INSIGHT ANALYSIS
    APPENDIX 3: FUTURE MARKET ASSESSMENT
    APPENDIX 4: COMPETITIVE LANDSCAPE
    APPENDIX 5: STRATEGIC OPTIONS CONSIDERED

AN OUTLINE STRUCTURE FOR THE IN-LINE PRODUCT 'BRAND PLAN'

With in-line products I am all for PowerPoint templates being the way in which the plan is presented. You will need to have available separately the strategic analysis leading to the decisions that have been taken and/or recommendations. Table B(2) gives my thoughts on what this slide deck should contain.

TABLE B (2)   EXAMPLE SLIDE CONTENT

Content	Supporting process/thinking

Business vision (strategic objectives)
    Quantitative objectives
    Qualitative objectives
	Definition of the market that you are in
	Approach to segmentation
	Sizing of these segments (i.e. their attractiveness)
	Our competitive position today – how easy is this going to be to maintain or improve?

Strategy for achieving the vision
    Which products, to which customers, to which needs
    The key strategic issues
	Which opportunities to focus on, using which product(s)
	Which customers to focus on/influence to capture the opportunity
	The potential barriers and which ones need to be actively managed

Plan to implement strategy
    Where and in what do we need to invest?
    How much do we need to invest?
    How have we built in what we learnt from last year's activities?
	What is going to be critical to success?
	Where you need to be by the end of the year to be successful
	What we learned last year
	Which activities need to be implemented to get there
	How we have ensured that the activities are consistent with and reinforce core brand values

Plan to evaluate strategy and implementation Did we achieve what we set out to achieve?	How we will judge our performance Which assumptions have we made Where are the risks? Other than sales and market performance indicators, how are we going to know that we are being effective?

Index

advertising 137

analysis *see* external analysis; internal analysis

assets 36, 38, 41, 108

attitudes 41, 109

behavioural analysis 33, 34, 39

beliefs 34, 36, 41, 109

brand 41, 68, 75, 109

    association 41, 109

    attributes 36

    audit 33, 36, 37, 41, 109

    central team vs. local markets 148–51

    challenges

        approach to building brand 147

        managing consistency in communications 147

        time to develop/milk brand 147

    choice 11

    definitions 1

    essence 62, 70

    function 75

    global 4–6

    health 143

    identity 75

    knowledge management strategies

        appropriating knowledge 145

        expanding knowledge 145

        leveraging knowledge that exists 145

    position 63, 75, 76

    product vs. company 2

    profile 41

    promise 75

    responsibility

        brand champions 140

        business management teams 140

        global brand manager 140

        global brand teams 140

    targeting 148

    values 64, 70, 76

        definition 62–3

    whole organization support 151–3

brand plan

    development 122

        avoiding costly mistakes 122

        cost out tactics 123

        exploring alternatives 122

        get group of people together 122

        increasing efficiency of marketing expenditure 122

        look at next year's non-financial objectives 123

        marketing programme checklist 123, 124

        review last year's CSFs 122–3

        strategic/tactical options 123

        tactics 123

    frequently asked questions

        choosing communication channel 124

        contact efficiency 124

        marketing mix 124–5

    integrated marketing communication (IMC)

        effect on design/development 120

    key components

        critical success factors 117

        four Ps 118–19

        marketing programme 118

        mechanism for monitoring/control 120

        non-financial objectives 118

    making communication work 120

        exhibitions 121–2

        promotion 121

        public relations (PR) 120–21

        sponsorship 121

    purpose 17

    skill improvement activity 125

brand situation

    challenges

changes to make 101
company process 101
customer vs. company perspective 101
frequently asked questions
classification of opportunities/threats 107
focus on target need-state/patient
segments 108
future trend/in existence 107
insight/understanding represents
opportunity/threat 107
physician/everyone's perspective 108
strengths/weaknesses from customer's
perspective 108
maximize market research 106
brand discrimination 107
customer insight 106
indirect methods 106
keep open mind 106
perceptual dimensions 106–7
scaling 106
review approach
adjustments to patient flow 101–2
focus on prescribing decision 102
focus on target need-state 101
future prospects 102
guidelines for opportunities/threats 102–4
guidelines for strengths/weaknesses 104–6
skill improvement activity 108
terminology 108–9
understanding
opportunities/threats 99
strengths/weaknesses 99–100
what is deliverable 101
brand strategy 75–6
brand position statement
framework 65–7
product promise 67
reason to believe 68
definitions 62–3
development 68
always start with customer 68
brand essence 70
conceptual target 68–9
core brand values 70
identify associations 69–70
position statement 70–71
frequently asked questions
brand position 75

common traps 74
customer need/insight 75
normative benefits 75
implementation 71
branding elements 72–3
key ingredients 63
brand essence 64
brand position statement 64, 65–8
conceptual target 64
core brand values 64
critical insight 64
key messages 64
market research 73–4
skill improvement activity 75
terminology 75–6
branding
definition 2–3
elements 76
importance to industry 3–4
reasons
influence on decision-makers 4
market share 4
opportunity to differentiate 3
value creation 4
responsibility
marketers 140
middle managers 140
senior management 139–40
budgets *see* sales forecast
building brands
channel selection 127, 128
effective communication
angry advertising 137
being trendy 137
do not make unsupportable claim 137
own unique identity 137
put logo everywhere 137
relevant imagery 137
frequently asked questions
in charge of brand 140
common mistakes 137
communicate several messages 138
effective/memorable campaigns 138
marketing mix 138
new/existing customers 138
responsibility for branding 139–40
implications 133
integrated communication development

analysis 134

appropriate research 134

brief agency 134

customer insight 134

evaluate creative idea 136

secure creative idea 134–6

test several executions of creative idea 136

testing process 136

skill improvement activity 141

terminology 141

communication 120–22

process analysis 134–7, 141

competition 23, 30, 98, 144

competitor

analysis 21, 30

performance 33, 35, 39–40

conceptual target 64, 76

critical

insight 64, 76

uncertainties 25, 27, 30

critical success factors (CSFs) 79, 85, 112–13,
        116, 117, 127, 129

customer

focus 147

insight 141

decision phases 30, 98

emotional insights 76

exhibitions 121

event plan

anticipate competitor activity 122

event signage 121–2

link to brand strategy 122

product availability 121

special/preferential treatment 122

external analysis

approaches

competitors 23

completion exercise 27

decision areas 22

decision point insights 23–4

evaluate key trends/critical uncertainty
    25–6

impact of events 26

interpret opportunities/threats 24, 25

list future events 24

losing/retaining patients 22–3

patient flow 22

reasons for interpretation 26

sales data 23

summarize understanding of situation 24

definition 19

deliverables 19

frequently asked questions

classification of opportunity/threat 29

future/in existence trend 29

insight as opportunity/threat 28

thinking through implications 29

what is an insight 28

key ingredients

competitors 21

patient flow 20–21

trends 21

skill improvement activity 29

terminology 30–31

see also internal analysis

Five Forces model (Porter) 30

forecast 131

see also sales forecast

Four Ps

place strategy 80, 119

price strategy 80, 118–19

product strategy 80, 118

promotion strategy 80, 119

frame of reference 65, 76

competitor 67

product class 66

product user 66

use/application 65–6

future market assessment 24, 30

implementation plan 85, 116

in-line product 89

brand plan 154

brand situation 100–9

central team vs. local markets 151

communication 133–41

implementation 117–25

monitoring/controlling implementation 143–6

sales forecast 126–31

setting new objectives 111–16

target segment(s) 90–8

insight 23–4, 28, 30, 64, 75, 76, 109

integrated marketing communications (IMC) 120
internal analysis
    approaches
        analyse data 33–4
        behavioural analysis 33
        brand audit 34, 36
        competitive situation 33
        competitor performance 33
        interpret findings 36
        needs/opportunities 38
        primary market research 33, 38–40
        summarize position 36, 38
        understand product attributes 36
    definition 32
    frequently asked questions
        need/attribute distinction 40
        physician perception of product 40
        target product profile 40
    key ingredients
        brand audit 33
        product audit 33
    skill improvement activity 40–41
    terminology 41
    see also external analysis

joined-up thinking
    example 50
    framework 44
        construct strategic decision grid 44–8
    frequently asked questions
        affect of weighting on segment
            attractiveness 51
        choice of opportunities 51
        limits/constraints of threats 51
    interpretation
        choose/identify opportunities 49–50
        identify key success factors 50
        strategic decision grid 49
        SWOT analysis 49
    reasons for 43
    skill improvement activity 51–2

liabilities 41

market
    analysis 30
    definition 18
    value 27, 30, 98

volume 26, 30, 98
market research 30, 33, 94, 98, 109
    guidelines 28, 38, 73–4
        behavioural analysis of competitors 39
        brand discrimination 39
        competitor brands 39
        indirect methods 39
        perceptual dimensions 39
        performance measurements 39–40
        scaling 39
market segmentation 148
    definition 11, 18
    frequently asked questions
        ask market research agency for advice 17
        indications in licence 16
        patient/physician needs 16
        reconsidering segmentation 17
        sales/prescription data 17
        study on patient/physician visits 16
        use of physician study 16
    market research 16
    planning 12
        define market 13–15
    skill improvement activity 17
    terminology 17–18
marketing
    effectiveness 144
    expenditure 122
    mix 124–5, 138
    programme 79, 84, 85, 116, 118
measures of success 85, 116
monitoring/controlling strategy
    achievement against non-financial objectives
        143
    behaviour 143
    brand health 143
    competition 144
    development
        analysis 144–5
        brand must benefit 145
        questionnaire/study design 144
        timing 145
    frequently asked questions
        resource allocation 145
        strong brand 146
        testing in the field 145–6
        tips 145
    key messages 143

marketing effectiveness 144

performance 143

skill improvement activity 146

needs 16, 17, 38, 40, 75

new product

brand plan 153

brand strategy development 62–76

central team vs local markets 148–51

external analysis 19–31

internal analysis 32–41

joined-up thinking 43–52

market segmentation 11–18

pre-launch plan 78–86

new product strategy

approaches

achieving objectives 55

capabilities 56

characteristics of each segment 55–6

clearly definable target 54

forecast 58–60

future market size/potential 55

investment 56, 57–8

objectives 54–5, 61

product competitiveness 56

questions to ask 55

summarize findings 56–7

definition 53

frequently asked questions

describing/evaluating options 60

key components 60

strategy/objective difference 60

types/levels of strategy 60

key ingredients

forecasting revenue/investment 54

objectives 54

options 54, 61

targeting 54, 61

skill improvement activity 60

terminology 61

non-financial objectives 79, 83–4, 86, 112–13, 116, 118

objectives 111

frequently asked questions

appropriate number of non-financial objectives 115

sales/market share 114

setting/measuring progress 115

maximize utility of market research

know where you are 114

tracking research 114

'new' non-financial

critical success factors (CSFs) 112–13

questions to ask 113

retain focus 113

setting 113

skill improvement activity 115

terminology 116

opportunity see SWOT (strengths, weaknesses, opportunities, threats) analysis

patient flow 20–21, 22, 31, 97, 98

PESTLE model 30

planning

in-line brand 154

new product 153

segmentation 13–15

strategic 131

see also pre-launch plan

points of parity 41, 109

Porter Model ('5 Forces') 30

potential 31, 98

consumers 11

drivers 41, 109

liabilities 109

pre-launch plan

development

cost out tactics 84

critical success factors 82–3

integrated marketing communications (IMC) 80–82

marketing programme checklist 84

objectives 83–4

skill improvement activity 85

difference with typical brand plan 78

frequently asked questions

how many non-financial objectives 84–5

repetition of objective 85

key components

critical success factors 79

four Ps 80

marketing programme 79

mechanism for monitoring/control 80

non-financial objectives 79, 83–4

terminology 85–6

value drivers 78
product *see* brand
promotion 121
public relations (PR) 120–21

reasons to believe 76

sales forecast
   frequently asked questions
      cut budget part way through year 131
      over/under budget 131
   operational
      budget preparation 129
      calculations 130
      competitive position 130
      level/timing of investment 130
      model adjustment 130
      plan investment 130
   skill improvement activity 131
   strategic 126–7
      approval of plan 127
      channel selection/building brand 127, 128
      cost per day 127
      critical success factors (CSFs) 127, 129
      investment implications 127
      market development 127
      market expansion 127
      patient opportunity 127
      patient retention 127
      patient share of class/category 127
   terminology 131
   types/importance 126
scaling 39, 106
segmentation *see* market segmentation
sponsorship 121
strategic decision grid 44–8, 49
strategy *see* brand strategy; monitoring/controlling
      strategy; new product strategy
strength *see* SWOT (strengths, weaknesses,
      opportunities, threats) analysis

success factors 41, 50, 109
SWOT (strengths, weakness, opportunities,
      threats) analysis 24, 25, 31, 38, 41, 49,
      51, 99–100, 109, 122

tactics 85
target market segment(s) 89, 98
   deliverables from analysis 90
   framework
      competitor analysis 90
      key trends analysis 90–91
      patient flow analysis 90
   frequently asked questions
      competitor performance 97
      data on segment 96–7
      patient flow 97
   maximize market research
      actual size of target 96
      potential of target 94
   review approach
      focus on facts 93
      market dynamics 94
      patient sub-groups 91
      update competitor market shares 94
      update patient numbers 91, 93
      update segment value 93–4
   skill improvement activity 97
   terminology 98
threat *see* SWOT (strengths, weaknesses,
      opportunities, threats) analysis
trends
   analysis 90–91
   evaluation 25–6
   external analysis 21
   future/in existence 29, 107
   key 21, 26, 30, 31, 35, 98
   underlying forecast 131

weaknesses *see* SWOT (strengths, weaknesses,
      opportunities, threats) analysis

About the Author

Janice MacLennan is the principal director of both St Clair Solutions, and St Clair Consulting.

St Clair Solutions is the organization behind the design, development and introduction of SCRxIBE – a leading strategic marketing planning tool. St Clair Consulting is a leading strategic marketing consultancy.

Smarter planning. Smarter results.

About SCRxIBE

The big idea underpinning SCRxIBE is that it facilitates the formulation of a winning brand strategy and an action plan that is focused on brand delivery. The tool itself is only as good as the insight that exists about the market in which you operate. SCRxIBE helps you organize this insight.

The approach within SCRxIBE embodies the principles established in this book *Brand Planning for the Pharmaceutical Industry*:

(a)   it provides structure to the analysis that needs to be undertaken
(b)   it facilitates strategic thinking
(c)   it enables the users to document (capture) discussion
(d)   it provides organizational memory
(e)   reports and PowerPoint presentations are automated.

St Clair

Thinking²

About St Clair Consulting

St Clair Consulting works with brand marketeers to provide structure to their thinking, facilitate strategic thinking, and bring clarity to their thinking with a view to helping them act decisively, and stay ahead of the competition.

St Clair is able to support the strategic marketing effort at every stage of a product's life cycle.